TO

FROM

DATE

DAILY PRAYERS

FOR

MY HUSBAND

DaySpring

Daily Prayers for My Husband

First Edition, January 2022

Published by:

DaySpring

Published by DaySpring, 501 Nelson Place, Nashville, TN 37214, USA. DaySpring is an imprint of HarperCollins Christian Publishing, Inc.

HarperCollins Publishers, Macken House, 39/40 Mayor Street Upper, Dublin 1, D01 C9W8, Ireland (https://www.harpercollins.com)

Written by: Lisa Stilwell
Cover Design by: Gayle Raymer

ISBN: 978-1-64870-328-7

Printed in Vietnam
26 27 28 29 30 QPV 10 9 8 7 6

CONTENTS

INTRODUCTION

Entrusting our spouses to God in prayer is the most valuable asset we have in marriage. Although people, obligations, and distractions often intervene, a marriage that is bathed in love and prayer will become the bedrock that helps us stand tall through it all. Prayer makes all the difference. No matter where you are on your marriage journey, remember that Jesus is the foundation of love marriage is built on. Talk to Him about your husband, daily!

These ninety short devotions and prayers will help you do just that. Be encouraged by the devotions, then make the prayers your own. Use your husband's name and pray with conviction and might. There is a topical index that allows you to pray for specific things in your marriage, or just go through from beginning to end for ninety days, as a way to stay close to God and build a stronger marriage. In ninety days, your foundation will be stronger than ever and so will your love for your husband.

Though the rain comes in torrents
and the floodwaters rise and
the winds beat against that house,
it won't collapse because
it is built on bedrock.

MATTHEW 7:25 NLT

THE MOMENT YOU SAID, "I DO"

Man shall leave his father and his mother and hold fast to his wife, and they shall become one flesh.

GENESIS 2:24 ESV

Whether you've been married a day, a year, or for most of your life, the journey and seasons in the future are always blessed when they are bathed in prayer. And sometimes the best place to start in prayer is with gratitude for when your marriage began—at the moment you said, "I do." It was then that you became united as one as Mr. and Mrs.

In the beginning of time, after six days of creating light and darkness, seas and earth, stars and galaxies, animals and man—God then created woman. He didn't want man to be alone. He doesn't want the two of you to be alone either. He is listening and ready to hear your prayers for guidance and peace, strength and patience, and especially of gratefulness and love.

Father, thank You for blessing me with such a good husband and the gift of marriage. You created him, and now I am blessed to spend the rest of my life with him. Help me to honor the vows I made on our wedding day. Help me to hold fast to him as he holds fast to me, no matter what we face today or in the years ahead. Show me ways to lift him up spiritually and emotionally so that he knows, without a doubt, just how much You and I both love him.

IN JESUS' NAME. AMEN.

DEDICATED TO ONE ANOTHER

Submit to one another out of reverence for Christ.

EPHESIANS 5:21 NLT

Sometimes loving and going along with your husband is the easiest thing to do, especially when all is well and going smoothly. Other times, it takes more effort, such as when miscommunication has occurred or imperfections keep needling your nerves. How does a wife acquiesce to her husband when her willingness feels overruled by anger or resentment or frustration? If ever there are times when a believer must "die to herself," it's during these times. Our calling as wives is not to be bowled over but to display the same humble attitude the Son had toward His Father to the point of dying on a cross. He understood the bigger purpose of His death and submitted to His Father's will.

God works through us most when we die to ourselves and yield, especially when it goes against our grain, not for our spouse's glory but for God's.

Lord, I love my husband and am devoted to him, but sometimes I need help—a lot of it. Help me to wade through all the thoughts and emotions that tell me to push back at him when You tell me to stand down. When push comes to shove, I don't want to fight; I want us to remain a strong bond for each other and for You. Give me the strength to follow Your example of submitting at a time when You wanted to walk away. Help me to keep Your bigger plan in view and to trust that You can and will work Your good in all circumstances, no matter how impossible they might seem. Soften my heart to Your Word, even when I struggle to follow Your commands.

TO YOU BE THE GLORY. AMEN.

A NEW BEGINNING

Light is sweet; how pleasant to see a new day dawning.

ECCLESIASTES 11:7 NLT

One of the exciting things you get to do as husband and wife is establish your lives together. That means developing your own ways of living, your own traditions—whether creating new ones or continuing old ones—your own ways of celebrating, and your own ways of working through trials. This can be challenging because it's natural to do something just because it's the way Mom and Dad always did it. It can even be tempting to turn to your parents for help. While it's good to seek wise counsel, you and your husband are bound to each other and meant to carry the aroma of your unique union. Establishing your new life together will be a process of trial and error, but hopefully it's one that brings intimacy, fulfillment, and a lot of joy.

Lord, I know that I am not my own. I belong to You and to my husband. I'm thankful for the gift of intimacy with him. I want to continually work to create and establish a life with him that is uniquely ours. Please protect us from any outside influence that might cause unrest or doubt between us. Join our hearts so that we are of the same mind, growing closer and stronger with each season. I want him to be the one I share my dreams and ideas with first and foremost. Help me to encourage his imagination and freedom to dream. Help us always be open with each other so that we are continually learning about each other and establishing a strong family mission that unifies us and holds us firmly in Your perfect will for our lives.

I PRAY THIS WITH THANKSGIVING AND PRAISE. AMEN.

UNITY OF THE SPIRIT

Be completely humble and gentle;
be patient, bearing with one another in love.
Make every effort to keep the unity of the Spirit
through the bond of peace.

EPHESIANS 4:2–3

It's easy to start thinking your spouse isn't necessarily playing on your team. Maybe he has a differing opinion or looks at the task from a completely different angle, and before you know it, it feels like you'll never be on the same page. The best way to thwart his attempts is to maintain "the unity of the Spirit through the bond of peace." But what does this mean? It means humbling yourself enough to refocus your individual agendas on what God wants. It means being patient the way you want others to be patient with you. It means eliminating anything that robs you of peace and bathing your marriage with prayer—together. Every day.

Father, I come to You in all humility with both palms up and ask that You show me anything that is coming between my husband and me and preventing us from having unity of spirit. Help him to do the same so that we will be one in the Spirit the way Your Word describes. Give us both the courage to be honest about anything that weighs on our hearts and creates a weak link in our bond. Give me patience—the same patience I know I want him to have with me. Give me a gentle spirit so that he feels safe and at ease to share anything with me that concerns him. Surround us; protect us both with Your peace—a peace that cannot be broken—so we will have the fullness of Your joy today.

IN JESUS' NAME. AMEN.

LET NO ONE SEPARATE

Let no one split apart what God has joined together.

MARK 10:9 NLT

When a man and a woman marry, the traditional ceremony is officiated by a pastor and witnessed by close family and friends. But God Himself is also there, orchestrating the power of His Spirit to join two individuals as one. It's a serious and emotional moment that runs deep and ought to be remembered as a pure and holy blessing from Him. It's a union to be cherished and protected from any outside force that causes the least bit of division. God wants us to be complete and whole—first as individuals, then as husband and wife. May your daily prayer together reinforce what He has joined.

Father, I'm aware of Your presence in my marriage, and I'm so grateful to know You are always a part of it. And I'm just as aware of our imperfections as humans. It's as though we finish a skirmish or a battle at the end of the day only to face a new one the next day. I need You to protect my husband and me from the outside forces that cause division. I pray for Your hand to be on him, to lead him into safe passage as he goes through this day. Please give us both discernment and a shared mindset to fight for each other and our marriage when opposition comes. We need You and the power we have in Your promises of favor and blessing when we trust in You.

IN JESUS' NAME. AMEN.

BE PATIENT

Love is patient.

I CORINTHIANS 13:4

Ah, patience. We all want others to be patient with us, but oftentimes, extending the same mercies toward our husbands can be unimaginably difficult, especially in conflict. That's because the definition of *patience* isn't simple—it has many layers. First, it means to go through pain or trials calmly, without complaining. Next, it means to refrain from lashing out while being provoked. Then, it also means not being impulsive in speech or action and remaining steadfast in adversity. Finally, *patience* means being willing to bear opposition. Of all the layers, to be *willing* could be the most important point of all. To be willing to remain calm, not complain, hold our tongues, and bear opposition means to sacrifice our own instincts. There's nothing about this that's easy, but by God's grace, it's possible.

Lord, having patience is not easy, and I know I need more of it. Help me to work on it one day at a time. Remind me the next time I feel my adrenaline rising to take a deep breath and call on Your name for help. I need Your Spirit in me to keep me composed and willing to choose a response that brings peace and calm when irritation or conflict comes. Please help my husband with this too. When I ask for his patience with me or our family, I pray he will be willing. Please give us both the desire and commitment to work on this together and the grace to remember how imperfect we are.

IN YOUR STRENGTH I PRAY. AMEN.

BE KIND

Love is kind.

I CORINTHIANS 13:4

There are many ways to show kindness to others, especially to your husband. After all, you know him better than anyone (except God), so you're able to be kind in ways that bore into the depths of his heart where an average kindness cannot go. Love seeks to be kind down to the smallest detail, whether it be a loving look, going out of your way to help, speaking choice words, sometimes withholding your words, waiting with patience, or praying for his welfare. The list can go on and on. God wouldn't have included kindness in His definition of love if it were not vital for a blessed and joyous union.

Lord, I want so much to be kind toward my husband—whatever I can do to make him feel joy in our relationship. Tell me, show me, nudge me to pick up on any cue for how I can make a difference in his day. I want him to know what a blessing he is to me. I want to be part of the reason he knows just how much he is loved. I can say, "I love you," but I want to show him the love I have through gestures that brighten his countenance and give him lasting peace. I also pray that You will shower Your kindness on him, in just the ways he needs. He is Your son, and I know You love him. Soften his heart to be sensitive to showing kindness to others as part of his witness for You, and help me to encourage him in this. You, Lord, are the epitome of kindness, even when we don't deserve it.

TO YOU BE ALL THE GLORY. AMEN.

LOVE CELEBRATES

Love . . . does not envy.

I CORINTHIANS 13:4

What? Envy your spouse? The thought may seem like a stretch, but there are many ways this feeling can ignite sudden emotions or create a simmering measure of resentment without you realizing it. Do people talk more openly with your husband than they do with you? Has he moved up in his job faster than you have? Is he more quick-witted than you? Does a child gravitate more to him than to you? There are many, many realities we all face in marriage that can cause envy, but Jesus equates an envious response to the absence of love. If this is a weak spot, go to God and share from your heart. Tell Him your struggle and ask for His help to love and be glad for your husband. And remember, all good gifts are from Him, no matter which one of you He chooses to send them through.

Lord, please examine my heart and show me any way I might be envious of my husband—then give me the courage to confess it to You for help and healing. I want the person he is and the milestones he accomplishes to be a cause for celebration and joy. Help me to always view him as Your child and to remember that You want to show him Your favor. Bless him in his walk with You, in the work of his hands, in his witness to others, and in reaching his goals that he's worked so hard to meet. Help me to remember that all the gifts and talents he possesses are from You. I don't ever want to be a hindrance to him accepting Your love for him. Thank You for giving him to me to love and to cherish and for the privilege of watching him grow and be blessed by You.

IN YOUR NAME I PRAY. AMEN.

BOAST IN WEAKNESS

Love . . . does not boast, it is not proud.

I CORINTHIANS 13:4

One of the strongest temptations everyone faces is to say the words "I told you so." Even thinking them can get us into trouble. That's because, for someone who was just proved wrong, those words pour salt on an open wound. When we're proven right at the end of a disagreement, it can feel like we've chalked up yet another conquest of ego-building accomplishments that rings the bell on our pride-o-meter. It makes us feel good, yet at the expense of someone else's pain and humility. And God clearly says that love is not proud—of anything. If we are to boast about anything, it is our weaknesses (see II Corinthians 11:30). They are gifts from God to keep us humble and our hearts soft toward one another, which is in line with the character of Christ.

Lord, give me a heart that embraces the reality that I am nothing without You. Who am I that You have even brought me this far (see II Samuel 7:18)? As I boast in my weakness, help me to elevate my husband when I'm with him so he will know without a doubt how proud I am of him. Help me to be quick to highlight his positive and lovely traits above anything I have done. Let him know that he is part of God's plan for my life. Help me to resist any temptation to say or do anything that would cause him anguish or hurt because my pride got in the way. I want him to flourish in all the ways You created him to be.

I LOVE YOU, LORD. AMEN.

LOVE HONORS

[Love] does not dishonor others.

I CORINTHIANS 13:5

The act of honoring others is so important for morale. Companies honor certain employees by acknowledging their excellent work and achievements, which brings joy and celebration for everyone on the team. When this happens, others are inspired to do their best and work even harder at improving their skills and putting their hearts into whatever they do. So why shouldn't this happen within marriage and family, especially between wife and husband? To honor your husband is to love him in ways that build esteem and show respect, which we all need.

Father, I want to honor my husband. His wishes, his requests, his desires—help me to see them all as being important. How can I recognize him as my better half and as being of high position in our marriage? May my words and actions and prayers cause him to feel respected and loved the way he should feel. Nudge me to stop and give him credit where it is due. I want him to feel celebrated for who he is and all that he does. I want him to know that it is an honor for me to even be seen with him, let alone be married to him. Whatever ways he might feel insecure or lowly, move in his mind and heart so he knows that we both view him in high regard. Help me to help him feel exceptional as my husband, because he is a work of art, created by Your hands.

IN JESUS' NAME. AMEN.

A SERVANT'S HEART

[Love] is not self-seeking.

I CORINTHIANS 13:5

Jesus, God's own Son, came to earth in the form of a man . . . to serve. And that's what He did—to the point of dying on a cross for our sins. He taught, He listened, He prayed, and He spoke truth. He healed, He multiplied food, and He knelt and washed His disciples' feet. His life here was the ultimate life for us to follow in order to know our Creator, to build our faith, and to know how to serve Him. The more we serve, the more we become a shining light in our communities. When we serve in marriage, we are not only a blessing to our spouse but also to the Lord.

Father, give me a heart like Jesus' heart; give me a servant's heart. Condition my mind to seek and serve to the best interests of others, especially my husband. I want him to see You in me so that love will grow. Help me to trust that You know what I need and that You will meet those needs as I focus on meeting his the best that I can. Make me attentive to the times when he serves me—as a husband, a friend, a confidant, and a helpmate—and to recognize him for them. I want him to know that his efforts are appreciated and not taken for granted. Humble my heart to be like Yours so that love will flourish in our marriage.

IN YOUR NAME I PRAY. AMEN.

BE SLOW TO ANGER

[Love] is not easily angered.

I CORINTHIANS 13:5

Being slow to anger can be very challenging at times. It requires patience and self-control to discipline our emotions not to react quickly and harshly. Even with all the persecution, lies, hatred, and taunting Jesus experienced, He rarely responded in anger. He wouldn't take the bait. He also kept love, not retaliation, at the forefront of His actions. Anger is not bad or wrong—it's an emotion God created us to have. But a lack of restraint and discernment about when to let it surface can be damaging. Oh, that we may strive to be as slow to anger as Jesus is, no matter how often our anger is provoked.

Father, I know that learning to be slow to anger is a process, but it's a trait I want to develop. Help me to keep love, not retribution, at the core of my actions. Most of all, I don't want to say or do anything in anger that would hurt my husband and cause further division. Help my mindset to be one of fighting for us, not against him. Give me the desire and self-discipline to talk through our problems amicably or not say anything at all and be a better listener. Help me to stay calm in order for us both to stay calm. Thank You for being the supreme example to follow; now help me to take on more of Your character the next time I'm tempted to lose control.

IN YOUR NAME AND GRACE I PRAY.
AMEN.

KEEP A RECORD OF RIGHTS

[Love] keeps no record of wrongs.

I CORINTHIANS 13:5

Our memories have incredible capabilities, especially when it comes to keeping a record of wrongs. Our minds don't necessarily record the wrongs *we* do—no, those go into auto-erase. But when it comes to the wrongs of our spouses, they tend to pop up at the exact moment we are angered or feel challenged to extend grace and give a blessing. Recalling wrongs doesn't require any special talent—it's a natural reaction, usually when we're hurt and want to hurt back. Thank goodness our loving God doesn't do this to us. He knows *every* wrong we've committed, and yet, by His grace and forgiveness, our records are clean. Let us extend the same grace to one another.

Lord, instead of keeping a record of my husband's wrongs, help me to keep a record of his rights—the good he does, the love he shows, the help he gives, the friend he is, and the faith he has. In fact, help me to think of one now to hold on to so that the very next time I'm tempted to bring up a wrong, a right will come out of my mouth. I can't imagine how many wrongs I've committed that You could keep record of, but because of Your forgiveness, You don't, and I am so grateful. Show me any areas I need to forgive. Help me to remember that my husband is not perfect, and that neither am I. With Your help, I want us both to work together on highlighting what is good and lovely and right in our relationship. I truly believe this will be possible through You, Jesus, who gives us the strength.

ALL PRAISE BE TO YOU. AMEN.

REJOICE IN TRUTH

Love finds no joy in unrighteousness
but rejoices in the truth.

I CORINTHIANS 13:6 CSB

There's a saying about truth that goes like this: "A half-truth is a whole lie." It's true, and where any ounce of falsehood exists, love will not be complete. In truth we find real freedom, and when we are free, we can have joy to the fullest—in life, in purpose, and in marriage. God's Word says, "[The devil] is a liar and the father of lies" (John 8:44). Any kind of a lie is not of God. So when we give in to telling a lie, or allowing a lie by withholding the truth, the father of lies is the one being honored, not our heavenly Father or our spouse.

Search me, O God, and know my heart; see if there is any offensive or untruthful way in me (see Psalm 139:23–24). Show me any part of a lie that may exist in my life. I want to be clean and truthful, trustworthy and free from the burden that falsehood brings. I pray also for my husband, that You would convict him of any area in his heart where he may be living in or holding on to a lie. Give us both a spirit of grace and readiness to speak with integrity and honesty with each other at all times. Don't let the father of lies have any place within us or between us. I want us both, as husband and wife, to live in complete freedom and rejoice in all truth, with nothing to hide. May Your Spirit of truth be with us always.

BLESSED BE YOUR NAME, GOD. AMEN.

PROTECTION IS A PRAYER AWAY

[Love] always protects.

I CORINTHIANS 13:7

When we think of the word *protect*, we usually think first of physical protection, but our minds, our hearts, and our spirits also need protection. When someone's mind is protected, it remains steadfast and at peace no matter what has attacked it. When someone's heart is protected, it remains soft when faced with bitter disappointment. When the spirit is protected, the joy of hope remains while dealing with hopeless situations. God's love is the ultimate protection any one of us will ever have, and a wife's love for her husband will include protection for him from the inside out.

Father, I pray a hedge of protection around my husband today. Surround him with Your army of angels while he walks, drives, works, and rests. Keep him from harm or injury; hold him in Your hand of love. Guard his mind from negative thoughts that weigh him down and rob him of Your joy. Help him to take his thoughts captive for You by recalling Your promises to bless and keep him. Keep watch over his heart so it remains tender and secure no matter what disappointments or unpleasantness he faces. Shield his spirit from discouragement so that his hope in You remains steadfast and strong. Cover him with Your grace and lift his spirits to be near to You all day long.

IN YOUR HOLY NAME I PRAY. AMEN.

TRUST—
THE TIE THAT BINDS

[Love] always trusts.

I CORINTHIANS 13:7

One of the beautiful things about children is the amount of automatic trust they have that they'll be cared for and loved. But by the time they become adults, the bond of trust in others has been broken enough times that it doesn't come so easily. Instead of being automatic, trust must be proven and earned—sometimes over and over again. This cycle often creates a challenge within marriage. Trust is one of the most vital cords that ties and binds two people together. Without it, doubt creeps in and insecurity brews. With it, security becomes a pillar of strength needed for a sound, thriving relationship. And when a husband and wife trust together in God—who is completely trustworthy—they have a stalwart chance at success.

Dear Lord, I want to trust You in all things—in my life and in my marriage. I entrust the two of us as husband and wife to You—for safety, provision, well-being, and love. Show me any ways I fall short so I can work on correcting them to bring reassurance and strength to my marriage. Help me not to do anything that will break the trust my husband has in me. I also pray that his trust in You will deepen. I pray that he sees the evidence of Your presence in his life to the point where he can completely rest in knowing You're in control of every detail. Help us to communicate honestly with each other about any areas of insecurity; then help us work together in ways that bring healing and encouragement. Remove any misunderstandings and replace them with Your truth. Help us to stay focused on trusting You together so that our love can flourish and stay strong.

IN JESUS' NAME. AMEN.

HOPE IN HIM

[Love] always hopes.

I CORINTHIANS 13:7

We all need hope. Without it, darkness enters, whether in our thoughts and emotions, in our spirits and wills, or even in our physical bodies. But with it, we're able to thrive indefinitely, no matter how dire the circumstances. Hope is a gift God gives us as we work, fight, and crawl through difficult times—and every marriage has difficult times. When a husband and wife aren't necessarily holding on to each other, they can hold on to hope—that God is with them and will help—even while the storm rages and they wait for healing. When all else fails and we don't know what to do, we can turn to the hope of Jesus Christ for each day and for eternity.

Lord, thank You for the hope I have in You. Thank You for being the reason for my hope in a chaotic and crazy world. And thank You for the hope I am able to share with my husband. Will you bless him with an ever-present, steadfast hope—for healing wherever he hurts, for a bright future when days are dark, for the fulfillment of dreams You've given him, and for the ability to press on regardless of his circumstances? Help us both to keep our hope in You, not in having perfect conditions, attaining certain things or material possessions, or having a full bank account. Help us both to begin each day and come together each night with a unity of spirit that keeps love and hope strong within our marriage. We need You and the endless hope that only You can give.

IN JESUS' NAME. AMEN.

PRESS ON

[Love] always perseveres.

I CORINTHIANS 13:7

Trials are inevitable—in our work, in our families, and in our marriages. Jesus said as much so we wouldn't be surprised when trials come (see John 16:33). But Peter said to be very glad in them because "these trials make you partners with Christ in His suffering" (I Peter 4:13 NLT). We can feel as though God has abandoned us when we struggle, especially when we've persevered for months, even years. But Jesus is our partner in suffering, and just as He looked beyond His pain and persecution and kept His eyes on the love of His Father, we are called to do the same. Let us keep our gaze on His love, not on ourselves or our trials, one day at a time—and press on.

Father, I lift up my husband to You and pray that he knows, without a doubt, that You love him and that You are with him. As he wades through the pressures around him today, help him to see Your love behind them, working on his behalf. I pray that he senses the partnership of Your Spirit within him as he works through his personal struggles as well as ours as husband and wife. Help me to do the same so that, while we may not agree on certain things, we can still agree to remain steadfast in our love for each other and for You. Help us both to keep perseverance part of our commitment to You and to each other no matter what we face.

ALL GLORY TO YOU. AMEN.

GOD NEVER FAILS

Love never fails.

I CORINTHIANS 13:8

Early in life we learn that if we do certain "good" behaviors, we receive a reward. If we have bad behavior, we not only don't get a reward, we often suffer consequences. What does this have to do with love? We tend to love someone only when they are nice and act the way we want them to. But when that person fails to do what we want, when they become hard to love, we tend to withhold our love. Thank goodness our heavenly Father doesn't do this—otherwise we'd all be without His love! He is perfect at hating bad deeds while still loving the person. The bottom line is God is love—they are one and the same—and His love never fails. *Never* is a pretty strong absolute, but He keeps the bar high, and aren't you glad?

Lord, thank You for Your unending, constant love for me and for my husband. Help me to pour my love into his heart the way You do—in ways that cover him completely, imperfections and all. Help me not to put conditions on my love for him. Help me to remember that we are all a work in progress—including me—and that Your love is the very glue that sustains us through our challenges on this earth. Your love is what blesses us and keeps us grounded each day. Where we fail, may Your love and grace rush in to pick us up so we can keep going. May Your love be our strength for holding on— to You and to each other.

THANK YOU FOR YOUR UNFAILING LOVE. AMEN.

NOT ALWAYS FINE

A time to be silent and a time to speak.

ECCLESIASTES 3:7

When someone asks how we're doing, most of us are guilty of automatically putting on a fake smile and saying, "I'm fine," when the reality is we're far from it. Most of the time it works, and we're off the hook for sharing what's *really* going on. What's hard, though, is when we ask our spouse how they are and they say, "Fine," but we know they aren't. Sometimes they aren't ready to talk, and wondering when they will be ready can be unsettling. It's so important to make and keep the offer to listen whenever the time is right. God often nudges us to talk to Him, and we don't. He waits until we're ready—sometimes for years—but His door is always open, and there's no time clock ticking.

Lord, I want to be a safe place for my husband to open his heart and share honestly about what concerns him. Help me to wait patiently for when he's ready, the same way You wait for me to be ready. Keep me sensitive toward him during times I know something isn't right and he's not at ease. Bend my ear to be a good listener, not only to what he says but also to what he doesn't say. Give me Your supernatural calm so I can soak in and take to heart any ways I can help or encourage him. Help me to be a friend he can turn to about whatever he needs or wants to discuss—the same friend I need him to be for me, and the same Friend You are to us both.

THANK YOU, JESUS. AMEN.

DWELL ON THESE THINGS

Whatever is true, whatever is honorable,
whatever is just, whatever is pure,
whatever is lovely, whatever is commendable—
if there is any moral excellence
and if there is anything praiseworthy—
dwell on these things.

PHILIPPIANS 4:8 CSB

There isn't a life that exists that's free of problems to solve, troubles to work through, and conflicts to settle. If we're not careful, our minds can become consumed with thinking about them and, eventually, become weighed down, sometimes even depressed. At times it takes a friend—or a wife—not only to help carry some of the burden but to help redirect a husband's thinking so his peaceful countenance returns and his outlook on life is put in its proper perspective. No matter what we face, we can remain strong with support from someone we love and when Christ remains at the center.

Father, I lift up my husband to You. When doubt, fear, or worry enters his mind, please help him to think about what is true—the truth that You are with him, You are for him, and You love him abundantly. Help him to think about what is honorable—the inner confidence he gains as he lives a godly life. Help him to think about whatever is just—the satisfaction that comes from knowing You see and reward upright actions. Help him to think about whatever is pure—the purity of Your love that pours from Your desire to bless him beyond measure. Help him to think about whatever is lovely—whatever brings a smile to his heart and joy to his eyes. Help him to think about whatever is commendable—the excellence in which he conducts the work of his hands. Help him to dwell on these things, Lord, so that no man, woman, inner compulsion, or outward force will rob him of the peace that is his when he does.

ALL PRAISE TO YOU. AMEN.

INTERCESSORY PRAYER

Jesus . . . is at the right hand of God and intercedes for us.

ROMANS 8:34 CSB

When words don't come easily, when we're faced with impending danger, when we're faithful—and even the times when we're not—we have a Savior who intercedes on our behalf before our Father in heaven. What a gift! If we are to be like Jesus, then we are to intercede for others in prayer as well, especially when they struggle. The power of prayer has no limits, and the scope of its effects probably won't be fully realized until we are in our eternal home. What a joy it will be when we can gather together to share all the miracles we experienced as our needs were met before we even knew we had any. We serve a mighty God.

Lord, as well as I know my husband, You know him even better. You know the number of hairs on his head, You know his heart, and You know his needs before he knows about them. I intercede for his best interests to be met to overflowing abundance. Send Your angels to protect him from harm. Guard his mind, body, and spirit from all attacks. Carry him when he is weak. Hold him when he needs comfort. Make Your presence known to him in just the ways he needs. Calm him and bring reassurance when he begins to doubt or worry. Clothe him with Your armor so his hope remains strong and the promises of Your Word are his defense. I entrust him to You and thank You for the blessing he is to me.

IN JESUS' NAME. AMEN.

REACH FORWARD

One thing I [Paul] do:
Forgetting what is behind and
reaching forward to what is ahead,
I pursue as my goal the prize promised
by God's heavenly call in Christ Jesus.

PHILIPPIANS 3:13–14 CSB

Paul's challenge to forget what was behind is a good one for us all. We often tend to dwell on our behavior and who we were before we believed and accepted Christ as our Savior, and doing that can be a stumbling block to our growth. We might even dwell on a slipup we made last week and wallow in our guilt, which can prove to be mentally exhausting. In his past, Paul's pursuit was to persecute, imprison, even kill Christians every chance possible, so just think of the guilt that could have weighed him down and hindered his testimony! But he determined not to let himself go back. He kept his effectiveness heightened by continually reaching forward in pursuit of his heavenly call. Christ died for our sins—we are *forgiven*. May we all move on and keep reaching forward.

Father, help my husband to look forward today—into Your light, Your grace, Your presence, and Your love. Remove any temptation he may have to recall past experiences that bother him and detract from being all-in on what he's doing today. Make him aware of any time he finds himself replaying something in his mind that has provoked anger or caused him pain. Help him to forgive whomever he needs to forgive, and let him embrace the forgiveness he has in You and the bright future You have planned for him. Help me not to bring up anything from his past except for memories that promote unity and love. I pray You protect his steps as he pursues his heavenly call and reaches for Your hand to lead the way.

IN YOUR GREAT NAME I PRAY. AMEN.

WHEN THINGS DON'T MAKE SENSE

Do not rely on your own understanding.

PROVERBS 3:5 CSB

It's hard not to rely on our own understanding of things. After all, God gave each of us a mind; aren't we supposed to use it? But we all experience things in life that make no sense whatsoever, and not being able to understand why they happen can keep us up all night. Sometimes we can feel bewildered, even afraid, about our current events. Relying on, leaning on, reacting based on our own understanding is really a misconception because we lack the ability to comprehend *anything* compared to God's ability and perspective. So why would we want to? Our sight is so limited, our minds are so small, it should actually be a comfort to release our demand to make sense of something and instead trust in God and remember that He knows and controls all things.

Lord, when times and circumstances get confusing for my husband, help him to stop and determine not to go down a road of analyzing and figuring out what You're up to. Remind him that You haven't gone anywhere and You haven't made any mistakes. Increase his faith to believe with confidence that You are working for his good. Keep his focus on trusting You in all things and acknowledging that You are always working out what's best for him, even when it doesn't make sense to him. Ease his mind and calm his nerves. Help me to reassure him of Your greatness in all things, even the things that he doesn't understand. Help him to hold on to the hope he has in Jesus and feel the comfort that is his when he gives his questions to You to answer as You choose. I'm so thankful that You are in control.

IN YOUR LOVE AND GRACE. AMEN.

HIS TRUE IDENTITY

Once you had no identity as a people; now you are God's people.

I PETER 2:10 NLT

Society is so focused on what we do for a living that our identity often becomes what we do, not who we are. This really hits home when we lose a job, can't perform the way we used to, or retire from a lifelong career. Previous accomplishments no longer matter, and the purpose we used to have that gave us a sense of value and worth is gone. If we don't fully grasp that our true identity is who we are in Christ—as God's child, as a family member of the most regal and royal King of all kings—we are lost. The purpose for our existence is giving God the glory due His name, not seeing how much money we can earn or which awards we will be given. Nothing on this earth compares to the status we hold because we are the ones God sacrificed His own Son for.

Father, I lift up my husband to You with thanksgiving for the person he is in You. I hope with all my heart that he knows full well that he is loved by You and by me, not because of what he does but because of who he is—Your creation and my partner for life. Please guard him from the trap of tying his worth to his accomplishments. I want him to know that he is valued, that he is a treasure that displays the work of Your hand. Guard him from thinking he is anything less than a holy one of the Most High (Daniel 7:18). I am blessed to call him my husband, and I thank You for such a gift.

ALL PRAISE TO YOU. AMEN.

HE IS A GUARD

His peace will guard your hearts and minds as you live in Christ Jesus.

PHILIPPIANS 4:7 NLT

Life today is so fast-paced and filled with pressure to do more and to be more. For men, it's all too easy to become overwhelmed and feel incompetent. Men often struggle to feel at peace with doing less and being less than the latest artist or business mogul on social media sites. The peace that Jesus provides can get diluted in all the chaos, which is why it's so important to be intentional about guarding our hearts and minds. We do this not just to keep the distractions out but to keep His peace in, which brings steadfastness and true rest for the soul.

Lord, I lift up my husband to You today. He has so many responsibilities that could easily overwhelm. I ask that Your peace will guard his heart and his mind as he goes about his day-to-day tasks. Help him to choose what's most important and let the rest go without worrying or feeling defeated or inadequate. Make Your presence undeniable so that he has a spirit of calm and joy no matter what happens. Help me, nudge me to give words of encouragement at just the right moments that will lift him up and safeguard him from any unnecessary pressure that he may feel. Please bless his efforts in whatever he does. I lift this prayer in Jesus' name and thank You that I am able to entrust my concerns for him to You.

AMEN.

HE'S INCREDIBLE!

For it was You who created [his] inward parts;
You knit [him] together in [his] mother's womb.
I will praise You because [he has] been
remarkably and wondrously made.
Your works are wondrous,
and I know this very well.

PSALM 139:13–14 CSB

Oftentimes people have a difficult time truly grasping and embracing the way God made them as incredible and wonderful. Unkind words we heard growing up, demeaning messages in society, and subliminal attacks on our outward appearance are all so difficult to overcome. Comparison destroys our opinions of ourselves. But God wants us to see ourselves in the positive, loving way He does. He does not want us to puff ourselves up with pride but to see ourselves in a way that allows us to thrive, grow, and use our gifts and talents for growing His kingdom.

*Lord, oh how I love my husband!
He is a handsome being created by Your
holy hand. As Your Word says, he is
"remarkably and wondrously made."
It is my sincere prayer that he knows this
for himself. I want so much for him to feel
valued for the incredible person he is,
just the way You made him. Please open
his eyes and help him to embrace
his unique and extraordinary qualities,
and to know, without a doubt, that he
is special not only to You but also to me.
Help me to inspire him to embrace these
truths for himself and to rest in our love.
There is no one like him, and I am grateful
to be his wife.*

THANK YOU, JESUS. AMEN.

A LITTLE GOES A LONG WAY

Let us pursue what promotes peace and what builds up one another.

ROMANS 14:19 CSB

Appreciation is so life-giving. We can work so hard that we come to the point of quitting from exhaustion, yet with one word of acknowledgment and praise, a fresh breeze of renewed energy can sweep in and keep us going. We all need to have our efforts noticed and audibly recognized, even if only on occasion. Saying "I see what you did" and "thank you" are small gestures that reap big rewards of love and peace in any marriage.

Lord, I am so busy most of the time between the work that needs to be done and the demands of life that it's easy for me to neglect to notice the little things my husband does for me and for others. Help me not to get so focused on what hasn't been done and to be more deliberate about showing appreciation for all the amazing things he has already done. Help me to see even the little things he does as grand. Give me a sensitive heart that notices his selfless actions and the words to thank him for them. I am so thankful for all the different ways he helps me and helps our home run smoothly. Don't let me take his time and energy for granted. Nudge me to stop and be truly thankful. I want him to know I value and love him more than anyone else besides You.

WITH ALL SINCERITY I PRAY. AMEN.

COMPLETE JOY

I [Jesus] speak these things in the world so that they may have My joy completed in them.

JOHN 17:13 CSB

Jesus wants us to have His joy so much that He included it in His final prayer to the Father before going to the cross. He knows that no matter how much joy we possess, it will never be complete without His promises and saving grace. Fear and doubt steal our joy and bring us down spiritually and emotionally. That's why it's vital to claim the joy that is ours for the taking and walk in the peace it gives.

Father, please watch over my husband as he faces many demands today. I understand the battle to hold on to joy when there are so many problems and distractions coming at us. I pray he senses Your presence all around and is able to walk in Your joy to the fullest, no matter what happens. Help him experience the delight that is his as Your son. No matter what negative thoughts cross his mind, I pray that Your promises will ring louder. Help me to never come between You and him in a way that would diminish any pleasure and comfort that You give. Instead, let me be a vessel for sending Your love and wonder his way so that I can be part of the blessing. Let gladness shine strong in every crevice of his heart.

IN JESUS' NAME. AMEN.

HE SEES HIS TEARS

I have heard your prayer; I have seen your tears. Look, I will heal you.

II KINGS 20:5 CSB

Sometimes when we hurt, we feel as though God isn't near. But He is—we just need reminding of His compassion and faithfulness to heal our wounds and lift our despair. A wife can be of great comfort to her husband during these times, but only to a certain degree. Ultimately, God is the final place of true healing and mending. So when you've done all you can to help, let God be your and your husband's strength. He sees his tears, and He hears your prayers on his behalf.

Father, my heart hurts for the things that hurt my husband, and I know that they ultimately hurt You too. There's only so much I can do for him in the moments he is filled with pain. I try my best, but my efforts aren't complete without Your help. You are the great comforter and healer, and I ask You to please hear his prayers, know when he is downcast, and heal his wounds. Touch him in a way that lifts his spirit and turns any sorrow into gladness. Wrap Your loving arms around him so that any anguish he feels will diminish. Mend his scars, renew his spirit, and give him hope so he can move forward in comfort and peace. Help me to be a strong sounding board and a comfort to him as well. I want him to be reassured of my love and care.

ALL GLORY TO YOU. AMEN.

EXPAND HIS TERRITORY

[Jabez] was the one who prayed to the God of Israel, "Oh, that You would bless me and expand my territory! Please be with me in all that I do, and keep me from all trouble and pain!" And God granted him his request.

I CHRONICLES 4:10 NLT

We all have dreams for our future. Some are small, and others will take a miracle from God to happen—but we serve a very big God. It's important to be able to share our dreams in a safe space where people won't say, "That's impossible," but, will give encouragement to keep dreaming and to take some steps of faith. There's no telling all that God will do when two people gather in His name and not only share a vision but also pray together for God's blessing on it.

Lord, I know my husband has dreams, both for himself and for our future together. You have blessed him with gifts and talents that he wants to develop. There are probably some he hasn't even discovered yet that will direct the course of even more dreams. Help me to help him grow in faith and take steps toward what You are calling him to do. Show me how I can encourage him in just the ways he needs. Help me to remain strong in my faith and not fall prey to thinking that his dreams are impossible. Please bless and expand his territory; be with him in all that he does. Keep his way steady. Keep him from discouragement; help him to be patient. Show me ways to inspire him and cheer him on and show him just how proud I am of the man and husband he is.

IN YOUR GREAT NAME. AMEN.

THE SWEETNESS OF FRIENDSHIP

As soon as [David] had finished speaking to Saul, the soul of Jonathan was knit to the soul of David, and Jonathan loved him as his own soul.

I SAMUEL 18:1 ESV

Close friends are needed throughout the ups and downs of life. Having someone to celebrate our joys or embrace during times of sorrow adds depth and meaning to even the dullest of days, not to mention the ones that bring us to our knees. While a wife's friendship is a gift, it doesn't replace the need for fellowship and special times just between men. After all, they have a language all their own that doesn't need interpreting or explaining. And when a man and his friend fill each other's cups, it's as if they get a new boost to face another day.

Father, I pray for my husband to have strong friendships that bring him fulfillment and joy. I pray for friends who will be a safe place for him to be himself and accepted just the way he is. I also pray for friends who will pray with him and for him, men who will stretch his faith in You and challenge him to be all they know he can be. Help him to be a good friend in return. I know it takes time to build close friendships, so give me the nudge to encourage him to take time away when You know he needs it. It's hard not to be selfish—I want him all to myself! But I know it's important for him to be filled with love from genuine friends—and other men of God—who care about his life and dreams, his frustrations and milestones. Most of all, help me to be his best friend ever—the one he wants to come home to and share with from his heart.

IN JESUS' NAME I PRAY. AMEN.

GROWING IN FAITH

Walk in a manner worthy of the Lord [displaying admirable character, moral courage, and personal integrity], to [fully] please Him in all things, bearing fruit in every good work and steadily growing in the knowledge of God [with deeper faith, clearer insight and fervent love for His precepts].

COLOSSIANS 1:10 AMP

Growing in faith isn't something a person does for a day, a season, or even a year; it's a lifelong journey. And on that journey, God makes sure we find ourselves in situations where a greater step of faith is the only thing that will get us through. How special to grow in faith with the ones we love, especially a husband. We don't always grow at the same pace, but oftentimes where one is weaker, the other is stronger. While it's easy to become envious of your husbands' spiritual growth or discouraged over your own failings, God often uses those differences as a tool to grow each of you in your walk with Him. The important thing is to embrace the shared experiences and celebrate together the triumphs that will surely come.

Lord, I pray that You would grow my husband's faith so he can be an ever-better witness for You. You know the plans You have for us, but I want to focus on the plans You have for him as Your son. Help me to be a daily reminder that he can move mountains with faith as small as a mustard seed. With You, nothing will be impossible for him, and I claim that promise for him now. Help his mind to stay focused on Your promises and his heart to be filled with a spirit of trust that comes with knowing You and dwelling in Your presence. Help my faith to be strong when his is weak. Show me ways to hold him up and fan the flame he has for You. Give him the courage to help me when I struggle with doubt or question my circumstances. Help me be a good reminder of the ways he has grown in the past and how sure I am of the victories we will share in our future.

IN JESUS' NAME I PRAY. AMEN.

OPEN MY EYES THAT I MAY SEE

Turn my eyes from looking at worthless things; and give me life in your ways.

PSALM 119:37 ESV

It seems that each new generation brings more screens, more television options, more social media channels, more news stations, and more places for our eyes to wander. We are constantly bombarded with pop-up ads and content these days, and it's easy to fall into the trap of paying attention to all the wrong things. It's an ongoing battle to keep our eyes on what matters and stop getting distracted with all the noise. It requires daily prayer for God's help. God honors us all when we strive to see life through His eyes, so He blesses wives who are realistic about the battle and take the need for His help seriously.

Father, please guard me—my eyes, my thoughts, my body language, and my footsteps. Help me take my thoughts captive to You and not fall prey to the distractions of this world. I want to honor my husband and our marriage vows in every way possible. I want him to feel secure in my love for him. Help me not to take delight in anything that does not please You. Please stand guard between me and anyone other than my husband, who is a treasure to me. I love You and I love my husband, and I thank You for blessing me with him.

IN YOUR POWER AND STRENGTH I PRAY. AMEN.

BE STILL WITH THE LORD

[Martha] had a sister named Mary, who also sat at the Lord's feet and was listening to what He said. But Martha was distracted by her many tasks.

LUKE 10:39–40 CSB

The pace of life is so fast, and we face constant pressure to perform more, create more, work more—and we do just that to the point of exhaustion. While it's good to be disciplined with the work of our hands, it's also vital to be still. Without connecting with God, acknowledging His greatness, seeking His wisdom, and remembering that we are not in control, we will have no way of knowing who He is or who we are in the scope of His purpose. The enemy keeps whispering, "Just do one more thing and you will feel satisfied." But no, the only thing that truly gratifies our souls is being with our God and relishing His presence.

Lord, I know how important it is to be still, yet my husband's schedule is full of demands pulling from all directions. Help him today to make time to spend with You and listen to what You have to say. You are his true source of strength, and he needs a lot of it with all that he handles. Help him to know You and trust You so completely that nothing can steal the assurance You give and the comfort it brings. I pray that his heart and mind remain anchored in Your truths no matter what interruptions may come. I pray that he is able to block out all other noise and focus on You. Help him to remember that Your promises are true and that he can call on You at any time. Thank You for the comfort I have knowing that You are with him, watching over his every move.

WITH A GRATEFUL HEART I PRAY.
AMEN.

PATIENCE AND A SOFT HEART

For whoever has [spiritual wisdom because he is receptive to God's word], to him more will be given, and he will be richly and abundantly supplied.

MATTHEW 13:12 AMP

Every day we are faced with decisions to make. Some are needed in an instant; others require a lot of thought, prayer, and picking apart because of the long-term consequences. Either way, it's comforting to know that God is aware of the smallest details and the desire of our hearts to make wise choices. It's challenging, however, when a husband and wife don't agree on which decision to make or the timing in which to make it. Having a soft heart to what God says and patience with the process and each other will lead to wisdom and favor.

Father, You know the decisions my husband and I are faced with, and few of them are simple or easy. Please empty both of our minds of our own agendas and fill them with Your Spirit of truth and wisdom. Open his mind to see my perspective and truly consider it, help me to be patient and willing to hear his thoughts with sincerity, and keep each of us pure and open to hear Your voice and follow Your lead. Help both of us not to get sidetracked, and remove any blindfold that keeps us from understanding or making wise decisions. Through it all, help us to make unity, love, and acceptance of each other our highest aim.

TO YOU BE ALL THE GLORY. AMEN.

PROBING QUESTIONS

The heart of a wise person instructs his mouth;
it adds learning to his speech.

PROVERBS 16:23 CSB

When two people disagree, they can find themselves in the fast lane to conflict and hurt in no time, so extra effort is needed to not go down that path. These wise words in Proverbs hit spot-on for controlling one's tongue rather than letting it spew: Instruct the mouth. Doing so, though, depends on the condition of your heart—it's got to want insight more than it wants to win. Disagreements oftentimes stem from misunderstandings, but it's hard to know without taking the time and thought to seek more information.

Lord, sometimes I just don't understand my husband—his thinking doesn't make sense to me. I need Your help to not jump to conclusions but instead ask more probing questions so I can understand his perspective. Put a guard over my mouth so I don't say something that minimizes or hurts him; bring to mind words that will edify him and improve clarity. Jesus had such control over His words and actions, and I want that same quality. Please turn my thoughts into Your thoughts so I have a greater sense of calm and patience. Convict me before I say something that will hinder our communication with each other. Help him to see that I am trying and truly desire to know his heart and the thoughts that he shares with me. Thank You for hearing my prayer, and thank You for being with us through this journey of marriage.

IN YOUR NAME I PRAY. AMEN.

IN QUIET CONFIDENCE

"You will be delivered by returning and resting; your strength will lie in quiet confidence."

ISAIAH 30:15 CSB

When troubles come into any given day, it's natural for our first response to be to hurry and fix things. Sometimes that works, but oftentimes it doesn't, and worry can take over. But God wants us to go to Him with our cares. When we do, His Spirit within us provides a supernatural strength beyond our understanding. But we must go to Him. Until we accept that we are not in control and acknowledge that He is, our efforts won't come close to fixing anything the way He can.

Lord, thank You for Your love—not just for me but for my husband. Thank You for all the ways You look after us, provide for us, and protect us while we're together and apart. Please be with him today. When he is faced with trouble, I pray that he will remember to turn to You first for help. Please instill in him the quiet confidence that is his when he walks in complete trust in You—for his care, his purpose, his safety, and all his needs down to the smallest detail. Wrap Your calming presence around him so that nothing hurtful or shameful will make its way into his thoughts or his heart. Help him to know without even trying that You love him and are his very present help in trouble. I ask and hope that You will be his stronghold and help him through any obstacles that come his way today. I pray this with complete trust and thanksgiving in You.

IN JESUS' NAME I PRAY. AMEN.

LEAD HIM INTO ALL TRUTH

He will guide you into all the truth.

JOHN 16:13

Deciding which direction to go can get so confusing. That's because we usually have multiple options to consider in any given situation, so it makes deciding hard. Should I go this way, or should I go that way? Should I take a step now, or should I wait? However, through it all we can be comforted just by knowing that when we ask God to guide us, He will. When we wait on Him to take the lead, He does. He wants the very best for us in all aspects of life, and He is faithful to guide us in His perfect time and His perfect way.

Father, I lift my husband up to You and ask that Your hand be on his mind, his heart, his body, and his spirit. I pray that when he calls out to You for direction or discernment that You would lead him to the truth of Your Word and the promises it contains. Keep the flame of his hope burning. May his heart continually look past his own logic and see the all-powerful and mighty God that You are. I pray that when he sees You he feels Your assurance and peace, no matter what he is facing. Whenever he feels confused, clear his thoughts to focus on nothing except what he knows is true—that You love him, You are with him, You are for him, and You are always working a bigger plan than what he can see. I claim Your promise to guide him into all the truth, which means You will guide him into Yourself, for You are truth. And wherever You are, there is freedom—freedom to rest in the fullness of Your love. I pray this for him with all my heart.

TO YOU BE ALL THE GLORY. AMEN.

LESS MEANS MORE

To live is Christ and to die is gain.

PHILIPPIANS 1:21

God is constantly working to grow and mature us as His disciples, and that work oftentimes involves discomfort, agitation, and even fear. That's because He has His perfect way of prodding us out of the comfort of our routines and steering us into circumstances that force us to depend on Him more than we did the day before. Every believer is a work in progress, both as married couples and as individuals. Growing in Christ is a matter of daily dying to ourselves and our own agendas, which can be scary and frustrating. Our reward is great, though: In living for Christ we find true joy more abundant than we ever thought possible. Less of us means more of Him.

Lord, as well as I know my husband, You know him better than anyone. You know the areas of his heart You want more of. I know it's not easy to give up old mindsets and habits—I certainly don't like the process—so I lift him up and pray he grows closer to You. I pray that he would live wholeheartedly in the trust he has in You. I pray that You would give him the courage to examine his heart and motives often so that they line up with Your plan for his life. Help me to be sensitive to his emotions and to be a safe place during the times he struggles and feels vulnerable. Help him to remember that You have his best interests and Your glory in mind.

IN YOUR LOVE I PRAY. AMEN.

REVERE THE LORD

The fear of the LORD is the beginning of knowledge.

PROVERBS 1:7

When trying to make a major decision and you're really not sure which path to take, uncertainty can feel like a dull knife trying to cut into your heart. The process can be agonizing, so you just want to get it over with. But you have a looming fear of unknown consequences, so you hesitate. God gives us clear direction on how to live a godly life, but the clarity can become foggy in the minute details of a married couple's life. One person might think they're sure God is pointing in one direction, while the other is sure He is saying to go in another. In those times, it's crucial to circle back to some of His basic truths: Revere Him, worship Him, and give Him the glory due His name. Often, when we step away from making a decision and what we want and get back to worshiping our Creator, He makes things clear and His answers come.

Father, help me and my husband to be still. Help us both to put aside our pleas and requests and get back to the most basic decision we can ever make together: to simply love You. Keep our love for You and for each other at the center of every decision, because we know that needs to come first. Clear away the voices that call us in different directions so that the only voice we hear is Yours. Remove our urgency to do anything other than to walk in Your Spirit, and keep our gaze on Your greatness. Help us both to wait on Your timing and Your direction, no matter how long it takes. Help us remain strong in the trust we have in You and the knowledge that You will lead us in the way You want us to go. Thank You for Your Word and the comfort we have knowing it will never steer us wrong.

IN YOUR GREAT NAME I PRAY. AMEN.

TRUST IN THE LORD

The fear of mankind is a snare, but the one who trusts in the Lord is protected.

PROVERBS 29:25 CSB

One of the biggest traps we can fall into is focusing on what other people think of us, both as individuals and as a couple. We want to have the appearance of being struggle-free and that all is blissfully well. Why do we do this, when no one and no marriage is perfect? The problem with this mindset is that our motive for acting the way we do comes from the fear of what others think—and what others think is flawed. Getting anyone's approval other than God's is a futile effort because none of us will ever measure up to ideals that constantly change and are often double standards. God's ways don't change—they are rock-solid, unwavering, and unfailing—and we can depend on Him without question.

Lord, it is easy to be concerned with what others think without even realizing it. Forgive me for the times I do this, and help my husband not to fall into this as well. Create in him a foundation in and commitment to You that is so strong that not a single person will be able to influence him more than You do. Work in his heart so that his motives stem from his love for You, not from fear of what someone else might think. Protect him from the attacks that try to undermine his trust in You. Remind us both every day to work and to live according to the truths in Your Word, which never change.

ALL GLORY TO YOU. AMEN.

HE IS IN ALL THINGS

"Now my soul is deeply troubled. Should I pray, 'Father, save me from this hour'? But this is the very reason I came! Father, bring glory to Your name."

JOHN 12:27–28 NLT

It's normal to want to flee from circumstances that are painful, especially when it's hard to hope. Jesus felt this way just before going to the cross. He was troubled and wanted to be saved from the excruciating, slow demise He was about to endure. But being saved from a valley experience isn't always God's answer. There are times when His purpose lies in the depths. Instead of fulfilling His desire to avoid the pain of His death, Jesus wanted His Father to be glorified and humanity to be saved. He knew His suffering would not be wasted—and neither is ours or our spouse's. God works for our good and His glory.

Lord, learning how to work through difficult circumstances sometimes feels bewildering—I don't always know what to do. Help my husband and me to keep our eyes on You. Help us to support each other and to reassure each other that we are not alone. No matter what comes our way, give us the resolve to stick together and lift each other up to go on. Remove any thoughts we might have of quitting on each other or on the life we've created together. Give us perseverance to remain firm in our vows to each other and to You. Help us to see the good around us and be grateful. Convict us to choose grace over perfection, because no one is perfect but You. Hold on to us as we commit to holding on to our marriage and our life together.

IN YOUR PERFECT WILL I PRAY. AMEN.

HE COMPLETES US

[God] put all things [in every realm] in subjection under Christ's feet, and appointed Him as [supreme and authoritative] head over all things in the church, which is His body, the fullness of Him who fills and completes all things in all [believers].

EPHESIANS 1:22–23 AMP

Going into marriage, many couples believe their spouse will fill most, if not all, of their needs. It doesn't take long to find out that this isn't the case, which can lead to disappointment and dissatisfaction. But God didn't create a husband or wife to be the other's all-in-all. If He did, we wouldn't need Him. He purposely made us in a way that we would never be satisfied and complete without His presence and provision—the kind only *He* can give. Not that this is an excuse for a husband and wife not to do all they can to love and serve each other, but it's a sober reminder not to expect something from the one we love that he or she was not made to satisfy.

Lord, sometimes I get frustrated because I know I'm not fulfilling every need my husband has. I try, but I know I fall short. I lift him up to You today and ask that You fill the empty spaces I cannot fill. Satisfy his longing to be heard in ways I'm not able to hear or understand. Speak to him with words You know he needs to hear, words of encouragement, conviction, guidance, or simply of Your love. Keep his heart soft when he gets frustrated with me. Please be patient with us as we navigate the places where we need Your grace to come down and fill us. Thank You for my husband and the unique and special man that he is. Help to make me worthy of his love.

IN JESUS' NAME. AMEN.

THE TIE THAT BINDS

Two are better than one because they have a good reward for their efforts. For if either falls, his companion can lift him up. . . . A cord of three strands is not easily broken.

ECCLESIASTES 4:9–10, 12 CSB

A husband-and-wife team working together to accomplish a goal, stand against opposition, or pursue a dream can be quite effective. There is twice the strength and brain power to make progress in a shorter period of time. But when the Lord is added to the equation, their "cord of three strands" can remain steadfast no matter the resistance or fray. The power of His Spirit is the bond that won't break and the inspiration to keep going. If either grows weak, He's the net that catches and the Companion who encourages. So whatever is on the agenda for each day, wrap yourself and your husband around the Father in heaven and look to His strength to go on.

Father, I want my marriage to be as strong as it can be. I want my husband to be as strong as he can be. I want us to be strong together in You. Be in our midst as we cling to You for all things. Fasten our hearts and lives to the promises in Your Word—the ones we need to thrive each day. Be a cord of safety and security when we are afraid. Be the vessel of knowledge and discernment we need to make wise decisions together. Be a thread of joy in us as we share in our trials and triumphs. Be the tie that binds us together so that nothing can separate.

IN YOUR HOLY NAME I PRAY. AMEN.

THE RIGHT BALANCE

His mouth is sweetness itself;
he is desirable in every way.
Such, O women of Jerusalem,
is my lover, my friend.

SONG OF SOLOMON 5:16 NLT

There are many levels of love a person can experience, and the love God has for us is the greatest we'll ever know. Sometimes, though, the love we feel for a spouse can be so great that, before we know it, God slips into second place for our time, our focus, our attention, our devotion. Love is one of the greatest gifts He gives us—He *is* love. So the best way we can love our other half is to grow our love for God first. The result is an unmistakable and overflowing rush of love between husband and wife that grows over time. God is the foundation that keeps our love sincere, sacrificial, pure, and steadfast—the very things that keep a marriage strong.

Father, sometimes the power my husband has over me is frightening—I feel vulnerable because I am so much in love with him. He is handsome, intoxicating, sometimes even addicting. It's as though he has me strung by his little finger and I'm helpless to get loose. I struggle at times to keep You at the center of my thoughts. He, and the love that we share, is a gift You've given, and I want to cherish him to the fullest. Help me to love You first and my husband second. I'm a better wife to him when You are at the center of my heart. I pray that You will protect the love we share from the world and all its enticements. Instill in us all that is pure and lovely for us to share with each other and with You.

THANK YOU, LORD. I LOVE YOU. AMEN.

TIME IN HIS WORD

Your word I have treasured and stored in my heart.

PSALM 119:11 AMP

Spending time in God's Word is one of the most important things any of us can do. The Bible is filled with promises from God, and reading it is the best way to get to know Him in an intimate way. Knowing God should be the ultimate goal of every believer. If we want guidance, we need to know Him. If we want answers, we need to know Him. If we want to learn about salvation, forgiveness, and the scope of His power, we need to know Him. If we want to truly understand the height, the depth, and the width of His love, we need to know Him. Learning His Word and praying are the best things we can do with our time.

Father, there are so many distractions, so many demands, so many interruptions to deal with each day. I pray a covering over the time my husband spends with You in prayer, in worship, and in reading Your Word. Give him rest at night so he's able to rise to spend time with You before the wheels of the day start to turn. Give him peace and quiet so that Your voice is the only one he hears. Speak to him through Your words and let them become treasures for him to carry in his heart and mind throughout the day. Lead him to the promises You know he needs in order to grow in Christ and build a strong faith. Bless him with the knowledge that he is a son of the King of kings. Fill him with Your peace—the peace that passes all understanding. I thank You and praise You for him.

IN JESUS' NAME I PRAY. AMEN.

HE GIVES PERFECT PEACE

You will keep in perfect peace
those whose minds are steadfast,
because they trust in You.

ISAIAH 26:3

With all the chaos in the world today, attaining peace can look like climbing Mount Everest. So the thought of having perfect peace simply by keeping our minds on God almost seems impossible, but it's true. As we focus on His faithfulness in the past and the fact that He has kept every promise He's ever made, how can we *not* believe with complete conviction that He will keep His promise of peace today? It doesn't matter the conditions, the season, or how hopeless the situation, He remains unchanged and ready to bless us with His peace. We merely have to look at Him and believe.

Father, I lift up my husband to You today with hope and a prayer that, whatever the day brings, his mind will remain fixed on You. I pray this promise in Isaiah over him, that You would keep him in perfect peace regardless of what he is facing. Open the eyes of his heart to see You and recognize Your presence in every circumstance. I pray he will see You in both ordinary and extraordinary ways. Open his mind to think outside any box that limits him so he is free to know full well that You can do far beyond anything he can imagine. I pray that he will trust You completely and know that You have already fulfilled any need that confronts him. Fill him with Your peace so that his spirit and mind are calm and at rest.

ALL GLORY I GIVE TO YOU. AMEN.

ON LEVEL GROUND

The path of the righteous is level;
You clear a straight path for the righteous.

ISAIAH 26:7 CSB

It's amazing how life can look one way on one day and completely different the next. Yesterday might have felt as though you were descending a mountainside of loose shale—one misstep, and you could fall. Today may feel as though you're driving on that same mountainside on a narrow, twisty road without a guardrail. So being able to do all there is to do—completing an assignment at work, facing a fear that keeps holding you back, or working through a major decision—and remain levelheaded on solid ground is something to welcome and embrace. And that is exactly what God promises when we look to Him and live for Him. Thanks be to God.

Lord, please be with my husband today as he navigates all the twists and turns and ups and downs of life. Bless the path before him so that each step he takes remains on solid, level ground, no matter the terrain. Guard him from taking any wrong turns. Keep him in the center of Your will, and keep him focused on what You want to accomplish through him today. Cover him with Your grace and keep his heart tranquil and unmoved because of the love You have for him. Pave the way before him in a way that he knows, without a doubt, that You are calling him in that direction. Light his path on the stretches where he cannot see. Hold him in Your righteous right hand and bless his efforts in all that he does.

IN YOUR GREAT NAME AND POWER
I PRAY. AMEN.

TURN TO HIM, LORD

*Answer me, O Lord, for Your lovingkindness
is sweet and good and comforting;
according to the greatness of Your compassion,
turn to me.*

PSALM 69:16 AMP

So often people imagine God as a task master with a rod in His hand. There are plenty of verses that speak of His anger and wrath (with good cause). Yet most of His Word is filled with the fact that He is loving and kind, softhearted and comforting. He showers on us the "greatness of His compassion" in full measure at just the times we need. When we come to Him with a sincere and humble heart, He doesn't hesitate to reassure us that He's near. What husband doesn't need these things? What a blessing to pray them over him.

Please turn to my husband today, Lord. Turn to him and fill him with Your great lovingkindness so that joy will be in his heart. Speak to him with words that remind him that You are with him wherever he goes. Hear his silent pleas, as well as his moments of gratitude, and respond with a rush of Your goodness and love that brings pleasure beyond description. Stir up his passion for You; kindle the flame of his devotion to You and to others whom he serves. Help him to simply enjoy Your embrace and revel in the fact that he belongs to You. Bless him and keep him in Your holy presence.

IN JESUS' NAME. AMEN.

DO NOT WORRY

That is why I tell you not to worry about everyday life—whether you have enough food and drink, or enough clothes to wear. Isn't life more than food, and your body more than clothing? Look at the birds. They don't plant or harvest or store food in barns, for your heavenly Father feeds them. And aren't you far more valuable to Him than they are?

MATTHEW 6:25-26 NLT

There isn't a single aspect of life that doesn't, at some point or another, cause someone to worry. It can creep up in our thoughts without us even realizing it. *What if I lose my job? What if I get sick? What if I can't pay the bills? What if I don't have enough to retire? What if I fail? What if [you fill in the blank]?* There are so many things to naturally worry about—when we trust in ourselves, that is. But when we turn our thoughts to Jesus and remember His command not to worry and, instead, remember our value in His eyes, our focus can quickly turn to trust in His provision and His care. We matter more to Him than anything—He proved that by sacrificing His Son. We can all rest in that.

Lord, I confess I struggle with worry at times, and so does my husband. Please help us to help each other not to. I specifically ask that You help me to be a good example in trusting You. You have been so faithful to us in the past; forgive me for not trusting You in the present. Help us both to simply take You at Your Word and not let our hearts be troubled (John 14:1). When he is weak in faith, let mine be strong. When I am discouraged, help him to be encouraging of Your provision. Bless our path together so that trusting You becomes second nature.

WITH PRAISE AND THANKSGIVING
I PRAY. AMEN.

A SAFE PLACE

Instead, speaking the truth in love, we will grow to become in every respect the mature body of him who is the head, that is, Christ.

EPHESIANS 4:15

Marriage is a two-person arrangement that provides a safe, comforting place for each spouse to find rest, hope, and encouragement. So what happens when a third party comes along? Maybe your husband tells his best friend a problem he has with you? Or maybe you're more invested with your parents than your husband? Of course, we all need trusting relationships and new experiences outside of our marriage, and these situations rarely arise out of bad intentions. It's only a problem when these third-party relationships drive you away from your spouse. In marriage, we are blessed to have a safe place to go to find help, comfort, truth, love, and support. Let's be sure to guard that sacred place, while we continue to find the right balance of external influences.

Lord, I lift up the safe place that my husband and I share and I ask You to guard it. Keep Your Spirit in us ignited and sensitive to anyone who may drive us away from each other, whether emotionally or physically. Guard our hearts and our steps from anyone who may intrude into our marriage and cause our relationship to struggle. Help us to clearly see any intruders and have the courage and faith to step back and turn to You. Help me to take him seriously when I meet someone he doesn't feel quite right about. Help me to respect the working of Your Spirit in him as a leader of our home so that we both remain in the safety of the shadow of Your wings. I'm so grateful we have You as our protector.

ALL PRAISE TO YOU. AMEN.

PRAY FOR ONE ANOTHER

Pray for one another.

JAMES 5:16 CSB

There's nothing like the privilege of praying for another person, to intercede on their behalf to the great and almighty God. He already knows what we need, but through prayer we often become more aware of what someone else needs. The power of Jesus in us leads our thoughts and words and opens our spiritual eyes for seeing beneath the surface of things. That's what Jesus did—He saw beyond the outer layer of attitudes and actions directly into the heart of each soul He encountered. Then He took His concerns straight to His Father on their behalf. We should all strive to do the same.

Jesus, I lift up my husband to You today and hope he can sense it. I love him so much, and I want him to know I pray for him throughout each day. Just as I can often tell when someone is praying for me, I want him to feel lifted and carried, empowered and loved through Your Spirit that is in us. You know his needs even better than I do, and I ask You to meet each one. Give him strength to accomplish tasks, help him have a clear mind for making decisions, and grant him satisfaction from the work of his hands. Go before him, behind him, and all around him with Your Spirit of love and protection. Fill his heart with Your joy, and let it abound no matter what happens in his day. Please give him encouragement, contentment, peace, and a desire for right living. I'm so grateful he is my husband, and I cherish his presence in my life.

ALL PRAISE BE TO YOU. AMEN.

HE IS GOD OVER BOTH

Enjoy prosperity while you can, but when hard times strike, realize that both come from God. Remember that nothing is certain in this life.

ECCLESIASTES 7:14 NLT

When we focus on how great, loving, and good our God is, it's hard to conceive that He not only blesses us beyond measure but also allows trials in our lives. Even more, because He knows the points of our faith that are weak, He'll use the heat and pressure in our lives to help us become more dependent on Him, and He'll strengthen our faith in the process. He works through our financial, physical, and mental setbacks to remind us that we are not in control and that we need Him more than we often acknowledge. Few things are certain in this life. Thankfully we have the promise of God's eternal presence and love.

Father, when I think of the trials my husband is going through, it's hard to think of them as good. But You are good and You are in control. Strengthen my faith so I can be an encouragement and helpmate in just the ways he needs. Hold him in Your right hand and bless him with reassurance as You shape, mold, and grow him into the disciple You want him to be. Help him to hold on to hope as he presses on, not knowing what the future holds but knowing You are for him. Help him to keep in view the greater purpose You are working out in his life for his good and Your glory.

ALL PRAISE BE TO YOU. AMEN.

A CLEAN SLATE

Let us draw near with a true heart in full assurance of faith, with our hearts sprinkled clean from an evil conscience and our bodies washed in pure water.

HEBREWS 10:22 CSB

There's nothing like a long, hot, soapy shower after a hard day's work to wash off all the dirt and grime. Not only does it feel good to the skin, but it's refreshing to the mind. The question is, though, when you're finished, would you put back on your dirty clothes? No, you'd reach for the clean ones. Likewise, when we accept Jesus as our Savior and the forgiveness He gives, He cleans and transforms us from the old person we were into a new creation. Knowing this, why do we often hold on to the dirt and grime from our past? He washes us clean—heart, mind, and soul. Let us draw near and hold on to Him in this full assurance looking forward.

Lord, I am guilty of rehashing past mistakes and offenses I've caused that weigh my spirit down. It's hard not to do. But I especially pray over my husband, for his mind to be clean and clear of this. Guard him from looking back at his failures and reliving the guilt from the past. Help my husband to gaze on You and the new creation he is in You. Help him to cling to Your steadfast love and the cleansing You provide when we trust in You. Help him to think and act and believe with all his heart in the fullness of Your love that resides in him. You have taken up residence in us, and there is no room for the past to remain.

ALL PRAISE AND GLORY TO YOU FOR LOVING US THE WAY YOU DO. AMEN.

TAKE TIME FOR SELF-CARE

[Jesus] said to [the apostles], "Come away by yourselves to a remote place and rest for a while." For many people were coming and going, and they did not even have time to eat. So they went away in the boat by themselves to a remote place.

MARK 6:31–32 CSB

On an aircraft, safety measures are given before takeoff. In the event of an emergency, parents are instructed to put their oxygen masks on first before helping their child put on theirs. At first this seems backward—it's only natural to want to help the helpless first. But looking at the bigger picture, if a father passes out while helping his child, neither one might survive. But if he helps himself first, he is then strong and able to help others. This is also true for a husband, whether he's a father or not. Because he can get spread so thin with constant demands, he must make time to rest and care for himself in order to be strong and lead his family in the best possible way. Jesus demonstrated as much for those closest to Him. It matters to Him that we take care of ourselves.

Lord, please open the gates to a peace-filled place for my husband to stop everything and be still. Part the pages of his calendar to make room for respite and rejuvenation, and show me how to help him make this happen sooner rather than later. You know him better than anyone, and You know the perfect surrounding that will take him away from the demands that swirl in his mind. Create the circumstances that allow him time alone to escape and be filled with peace. Show me what I can do to help, and I will do it. You know how much I love him and how I want the very best for his mind, body, and spirit. I love You, Lord, and ask Your blessing of rest on him now.

IN JESUS' NAME. AMEN.

FIND ENJOYMENT

Behold, what I have seen to be good and fitting is to eat and drink and find enjoyment in all the toil with which one toils under the sun the few days of his life that God has given him.

ECCLESIASTES 5:18 ESV

Life can be so repetitive. We get up, work, eat, go to bed, and do it all over again day after day. Statistics show that over 50 percent of people aren't satisfied in their jobs, yet we spend 30 percent of our lives "toiling under the sun." So when we *do* enjoy our labor, it is a true blessing. When we are doing what God has called us to do, we are able to use the gifts He's given us for a purpose greater than ourselves. The key is to learn what His will is—because He knows us better than anyone—and work at it with all our hearts.

Lord, I pray for the work of my husband's hands. Let whatever he accomplishes be satisfying to his soul. Bless him to experience what is good in even the smallest details he has to accomplish. Give him strength and clarity of mind for working efficiently and with ease. Stretch his mind to grow and learn new things that are gratifying to his heart. Build his confidence in ways that enable him to enjoy what he does and rest in satisfaction in his vocation. Show me how I can encourage and help him. Help him to reach the goal of a job well done at the end of each day.

IN JESUS' NAME I PRAY. AMEN.

TIME TO LAUGH

There is . . . a time to laugh.

ECCLESIASTES 3:1, 4

When asked their secret to staying together so long, many couples who are celebrating a milestone wedding anniversary will often say it's because they've kept their sense of humor. Laughing at yourself when you've made a mistake or seeing the humor in otherwise stressful times is medicine for the soul. Laughter is the lemonade that's made from lemons and a healing balm for hearts that are heavy. Laughing restores energy that otherwise would be used up by dwelling on problems. It's important to begin each day in quiet devotion to God and to end each day only after some amount of joy has bubbled up and burst out to those around us.

Father, thank You for the gift of joy, no matter our circumstances. Help me to tap into it the next time I start to take myself too seriously. Lighten my heart and give me eyes to see the humor that's all around that can easily go unnoticed. Bless my husband with a good, hearty laugh today too. Tickle him right where You know will bring a glow and a smile to his face. Give us both a bright spirit to enjoy each other and to live in joy together. Help us to remember to be of good cheer because we have each other—that is a wondrous blessing in itself.

ALL PRAISE BE TO YOU. AMEN.

LET MERCY FLOW

Surely goodness and mercy and unfailing love shall follow me all the days of my life.

PSALM 23:6 AMP

Anytime there's an ad that says something is free, it's natural to roll the eyeballs and shrug off the thought. Nothing in life is free—at least, that's what we're conditioned to think. We've got to read the fine print that discloses the *real* cost, because there's always a cost for something. This is why it's often hard to understand the full scope of the reality that God's mercy is free to us. It's free because His Son, Jesus, covered the cost for our sins—He took them all upon Himself at the cross. So when God's divine favor overtakes what we really deserve, it's natural to give thanks in all humility for such a gift and want to share it with others. Praise Him!

Father, I ask that You let Your goodness flow into my husband's heart. I want him to feel Your unmistakable and unfailing love, especially when he feels as though he doesn't deserve it. Please soften and open his heart to receive and accept the gift of Your mercy and healing. Let Your compassion envelop him as he works and serves You and others. Bless him and our marriage with a spirit of forbearance on the hard days and deep-seated joy on the good ones. May Your Spirit in him be a constant reminder for him to dwell not on mistakes in the past but instead on the beauty of the present. Give him a mindset that believes each moment is new and filled with opportunity. Go before him now and all the days of his life, and fill him with Your blessing of abundance and favor.

ALL PRAISE BE TO YOU. AMEN.

LIVE IN HARMONY

Rejoice with those who rejoice;
weep with those who weep.
Live in harmony with one another.
ROMANS 12:15–16 CSB

Family dynamics can be tricky, especially when it comes to siblings, in-laws, aunts, uncles, and cousins. We don't choose the family we're born into the way we choose a friend. Friends bear a commonality that produces harmony, joy, and, hopefully, accountability. Family members can be polar opposites, and envy can become a serious issue, such as when someone becomes upset over where you choose to spend Thanksgiving or Christmas. The bottom line is we are created to share experiences with one another—both the good and the bad—whether in our biological family, work family, or church family. God designed us to know the fullness that comes with sharing our joy during our high points and having compassion during times of difficulty. Joy and compassion are vital ingredients for living among extended family in a way that honors God.

Lord, I pray for my husband's relationships with his family and my relationships with mine. Even though we are our own family now, I know it's important to support our extended families both together and individually. Give us hearts of grace that covers any shortcomings and the will and desire to stay connected to our families and to continue to love them. Strengthen our bond with one another and heal any wounds that may linger. And when needed, help us to be quick to forgive so we can get back to experiencing life together. Thank You for family and the joys and sorrows we share. Thank You for the wisdom passed down from older generations and the heritage they have left for us to pass on to the next.

IN JESUS' NAME. AMEN.

BREATHE HIM IN

The Spirit of God has made me [Job],
and the breath of the Almighty gives me life.

JOB 33:4 CSB

We can all identify to some degree with the drawn-out season of loss and illness that Job experienced. Maybe not to the full extent he suffered, but at least in some part. No one is immune to misfortune and heartache that pull the rug out from under our feet, make us fall on our faces, and offer us no solution for getting back up. Job's example of holding on to hope has inspired many of us through troubled times. Day after day, he clung to the basics of his faith by acknowledging where his life came from: the very breath of God. Because of Him, we exist, and because of Him, we can breathe in new life to sustain and carry us through whatever we are facing—just like Job.

Lord, I lift up my husband to You today with a full heart. Instill in him a hope that won't die and the mindset to breathe You in for his very life, purpose, and direction. Show him that You're with him; speak Your love and assurance into his heart. Keep his flame for You burning regardless of trials he is facing. Remind him to breathe out the past to make room for the overflow of blessings that are both present and to come. Hear his cries for help and heal the wounds he bears. Help him to keep You front and center of his focus and not look to the left or to the right. Reward his righteousness with Your favor and peace. He is my lover and my friend, and I entrust him to You.

IN YOUR GREAT NAME I PRAY. AMEN.

LOOK UP

Unto You I lift up my eyes,
O You who are enthroned in the heavens!

PSALM 123:1 AMP

Have you ever noticed that directional signs are elevated above the busyness of people and things moving around on the earth? Road signs are above the traffic so we know which exit to take, and grocery signs are above each row of food so we know where to find what we need. The sky above shows signs of impending weather so we'll (sometimes) know how to dress for each day. But the greatest signs of all are in the array of stars, planets, and galaxies enthroned in the heavens. They are God's sovereign handiwork to remind us of His vast and great power beyond our feeble imaginations. When we look up—with our eyes, our hearts, and the hope we have in Him—we are reminded of the light of His love that's waiting to show us day by day which way to go.

Lord, I pray that whatever my husband faces today, he will look up—to You, Your love for him, Your presence, Your power, and Your faithfulness. If something or someone triggers worry or anxiety, may he look up to Your Word for instruction and for assurance. If someone blesses him with words of encouragement, may he look up to You, the Giver of all good things. If he finds himself in danger or a compromising position, may he look up to You for safety and protection in the shadow of Your wings. If he is filled with peace, may he look up to You in gratitude for Your peace that passes all understanding. I look up with him and worship You with thanksgiving and praise. Thank You for blessing me with him as my husband and brother in Christ. My heart overflows.

ALL PRAISE BE TO YOU. AMEN.

SELF-TALK

May the words of my mouth and the meditation of my heart be acceptable to You, Lord, my rock and my Redeemer.

PSALM 19:14 CSB

It's probably safe to say that when most people read this verse about the words of our mouths being acceptable to God, they think it applies to moments when we speak to or about other people. But it's also vital to remember that the words we speak to ourselves can make or break the spirit within us too. Can you identify? When was the last time you thought, *What am I doing here? I'm not as qualified as everyone else; I am inadequate; I can't believe I just blew it again. Why keep trying if I'm just going to mess up again?* The thoughts we think about ourselves are as important to God as the ones we think about others. The negative and positive self-talk affects how we perform at everything. It's hard to love on others when we talk ourselves down. So, may the words we speak and the meditations of our thoughts—whether about ourselves or others—be truly pleasing to God.

Oh, Lord, I can't read my husband's mind, but You know his every thought. You know the things he thinks about You, me, others, and himself. I pray that the meditations of his heart are pure and holy, positive, and filled with hope. I pray that he will fully embrace how amazing he is just the way he is. Guard his mind from thinking negative thoughts about himself. I want him to walk confidently in the truth that he was fearfully and wonderfully made by You. May he not miss hearing and receiving the loving words You say to him. Help my words to edify and honor him for the royal child, brother in Christ, and beloved husband that he is.

IN YOUR PRECIOUS NAME I PRAY.
AMEN.

BE THANKFUL . . . ALWAYS

Be thankful in all circumstances, for this is God's will for you who belong to Christ Jesus.

I THESSALONIANS 5:18 NLT

What? Be thankful in *all* circumstances? What if you just got laid off? What if your spouse is chronically ill? What if there isn't enough money to pay this month's bills? It seems pretty ridiculous to be thankful in these situations, yet it's what God tells us to do. The key is, He doesn't say to be thankful *for* all circumstances; He says to be thankful *in* them. We can give thanks for what He will show us about His faithfulness when we don't know what to do. We can give thanks for knowing He's in control and will provide for our every need—even when we can't see it. We can thank Him for the promise of His joy regardless of the torrents around us. And ultimately, we can be thankful for our salvation because of His Son. God has invested too much in us simply to leave us. We can be thankful in all circumstances because He is faithful in them all.

Father, You know full well the challenges my husband and I are facing. Yet I want to step out in faith and thank You for being in them with us. Thank You that we have each other as we walk this journey together. Thank You for what I am learning about Your faithfulness. I don't want to limit Your power and ability within my own mind. Help my heartfelt thanks be an influence for my husband to draw from. Help us to join together and look for all the good that You have faithfully put all around us, all because of You. Help us not to focus on all the "what ifs" that could overwhelm us. Help us to take our thoughts captive to Christ and walk in Your strength today.

IN JESUS' NAME I PRAY. AMEN.

SHINE BRIGHT!

Arise, shine, for your light has come,
and the glory of the Lord has risen upon you.

ISAIAH 60:1 ESV

Just as a TV streams light into a room when you're watching a movie, the Lord streams His glorious light through you to others. What a blessing and privilege that is! He calls His children to get up, go out, and spread His love so others will come to know Him and be reminded of His saving grace. There's no better place to begin shining His light than within a marriage covenant—by covering each other with the love of the Lord. From there, go out—whether to work or the store or simply a walk around the neighborhood—and spread God's love to others. This is our calling each day, and the boundaries are limitless. Possessing His life within us isn't designed to be a secret; it's to be shared for everyone to see and find for themselves.

Father, thank You for the abundant light and life I have in You. You are my hope, and I want to follow You every day. Help me to pour Your love onto my husband; make me a vessel of the love You and I have for him. Go with him today and spread Your goodness and grace onto whomever he meets. Let Your light in him be a magnet to draw others closer to You. Fill him with Your joy that comes when we live fully devoted to You and Your ways. Bless him with Your peace as he trusts in You and encourages others to do the same. Thank You for being our light of hope in a dark world.

ALL PRAISE TO YOU. AMEN.

PUT ON HIS ARMOR

Put on the full armor of God so that you can stand against the schemes of the devil. For our struggle is not against flesh and blood, but against the rulers, against the authorities, against the cosmic powers of this darkness, against evil, spiritual forces in the heavens.

EPHESIANS 6:11–12 CSB

While God works His kingdom purposes through individuals, He also works them within marriages. The journey a husband and wife take as they grow in faith together can be both exciting and challenging. It's exciting to witness firsthand the miracles God works in your spouse and experience His answers to prayers that are prayed together. It's challenging to persevere through the times when God seems far away and the answers don't come when we want them to. Those are the times when we feel attacked by a world doing all it can to destroy our faith—in God and each other. Thank goodness we have God's armor to cover and protect our hearts, minds, and spirits while we fight the good fight and fulfill His plan for our lives and His glory. We just have to remember to put it on.

Father, thank You for giving us access to the full armor of God. I am so weak and undeserving, but still You give me Your strength. Give me the desire to fight for what is right. Help me fight for my marriage and be a woman who continually chooses her husband. Help me fight for what is best for my husband. Give me the strength to live and love from a place of humility and grace. Help me be a constant source of light in my husband's life. Thank You for empowering me to live this way and choose a life of light.

AMEN.

PUT THE OTHER FIRST

Love one another deeply as brothers and sisters.
Take the lead in honoring one another.

ROMANS 12:10 CSB

We all have our own opinions, preferences, and processes for living through each day. If left to our own desires, we would plow forward with no thought to what our spouse prefers or how he would want to do things. But we are called to "honor [by] giving preference to one another." This means putting a spouse's needs and wants before our own. It's natural to think that when we do, we'll get left out, but God sees all things, and He rewards us when we walk in His ways and trust in His provision. Truly believing and giving preference to our husbands in faith brings to light the honor we show God by doing things His way.

Lord, I want to please You, and I want to please my husband. Give me a spirit and mindset to put his desires before mine, and help me to trust You to fulfill the desires You know I have. Help me to form the habit of making this a natural way of living and loving each day. Make me sensitive to my husband's preferences—the food he likes, the movies he watches, the activities he enjoys, and the music he listens to. I want to honor him in the ways that mean the most to him. Give me an attentive ear and eyes to see what brings him joy and makes his heart smile. I want to be a blessing by putting his inclinations at the forefront of my mind and heart.

IN YOUR STRENGTH AND GRACE
I PRAY. AMEN.

MAKE PEACE

Blessed are the peacemakers.

MATTHEW 5:9

Every husband and wife knows that it doesn't take much to destroy peace in a relationship. An argument can start out of nowhere, bringing with it harsh words, hurt feelings, and cards for keeping score. When disagreement erupts, the question then is, how do you get past the damage and back on a track of harmony? Jesus' words in this verse lead to the answer: be peacemakers, not fight winners. Peace doesn't happen all by itself. It takes effort to make it, and it usually begins with a sincere apology followed by asking for forgiveness for your part of the problem—and we all have a part. Then there's the act of extending forgiveness, the way Jesus provides forgiveness for us. Yes, when two people strive to be peacemakers, they are indeed blessed.

Father, first, thank You for forgiving me. I don't know where I'd be without Your forgiveness. Because I am forgiven, help me to extend the same grace to my husband when we have a conflict. Help me to work toward peace rather than wanting to win or make a point. Give me patience and eyes to see the bigger picture of why we even have conflict in the first place. I love my husband and want to live in harmony and share the goodness of life with him. Please soften his heart so that he is quick to forgive and remembers that we are on the same team. Free us both from the pride that comes from wanting our own way.

I HUMBLY ASK THIS IN YOUR NAME. AMEN.

WHICH ONE WILL YOU LOVE?

No one can serve two masters, since either he will hate one and love the other, or he will be devoted to one and despise the other. You cannot serve both God and money.

MATTHEW 6:24 CSB

Money—or how it's viewed—can be a tumultuous topic in marriage. Unless a husband and wife are of the same mind about it and how to handle it, there can be a lot of conflict. In this verse, Jesus reveals the most vital point to consider before handling money, and it lies at the core of our hearts: Do you love money or do you love God. He literally gives us an either/or choice—He doesn't say you can love both. Either we get up each day to work for the Lord on whatever purpose He's given us to fulfill or we get up each day to work for more money. It's a question each of us may have to ask every day in order to keep our priorities straight, but that's okay. God understands. He gave us this verse to help us stay on track.

Father, this question certainly hits at my core, especially during the times when I'm not sure how to pay all the bills. So I ask You first to help me keep my love for You as my motive for working each day. I also pray for my husband, that he, too, will keep his thoughts and motives fixed on living for You and serving You, with complete trust that You will meet our needs. My hope is that we have the same mind and heart in this. Help us both to view money as a tool that You give us to manage; it's not meant to replace You as our provider. May we both trust in You together. As we serve You, please bless us abundantly according to Your will for our lives.

IN YOUR GREAT NAME I PRAY. AMEN.

THE COMPARISON TRAP

I [Paul] have learned how to be content with whatever I have. I know how to live on almost nothing or with everything. I have learned the secret of living in every situation, whether it is with a full stomach or empty, with plenty or little.

PHILIPPIANS 4:11–12 NLT

It happened again: Your husband's coworker arrived with a brand-new Jeep, and now your husband is hinting at one, and they're expensive. Not long ago it was a friend who got a new ski boat, and before that, your neighbors booked a guided fishing trip in Alaska. It's hard to be content when people around us have things we want but can't have. But true contentment isn't found in what we have—it's found in the fulfillment we have in our relationship with Christ. The closer we are to Him, the more filled we become and the less drawn we are to what the world says will make us happy. Look at Paul—he wrote these wise words while sitting in a jail cell. He'd experienced it all, and in the end, his contentment relied not on outward circumstances or things but on the love that filled his heart each day for Jesus.

Lord, I pray a covering over our hearts and minds—that You would protect them from the comparison trap that's so easy to fall into. I pray that our love for You will grow, and as it does, that we would be so filled with Your love for us that we would draw on the kind of contentment that only You give. If my husband is to feel any restlessness, I pray it will be only because of the convictions You place in his heart for stretching and growing his faith. Help him to see Your good that's all around, and let it be his focus. You are the Giver of all good gifts, and I entrust the things we desire into Your hands to provide them—or not—if that's what You choose. May our love for You, and our love for each other, be enough, no matter our circumstances.

THANK YOU FOR YOUR ABUNDANCE AND LOVE. AMEN.

I TAKE YOU, MY PARTNER IN LIFE

The Lord God made the rib He had taken from the man into a woman and brought her to the man.

GENESIS 2:22 CSB

After God created the heavens and the earth, He brought Adam a gift that would change his life forever: Eve. And the holy blessing is that Adam received her with open arms. Such is what we do when someone gives us a gift—we receive it, we unwrap it, we look at it, and we hold on to not only the joy we feel from the gift but the sentiment we feel toward the giver. The excitement Adam must have felt, the gratefulness to God he must have expressed, is no less than what any husband experiences when God has "brought" him a lifelong partner. In turn, may you take and receive your husband not only the way you did on your wedding day but *every* day the sun rises, while holding on to the same gratitude you felt the day God brought him into your life.

Father, my heart overflows with sincere appreciation because You created and brought to me my husband, my partner in life. I remember the day we met and the day we said our vows, and I carry that joy into today. Help me to keep him and the blessing he is to me above the dailiness of life and the details that try to draw my eyes and my heart off such a gift. Help me to honor him, serve him, love him, laugh with him, cry with him, and forgive him throughout our days and years together. Help me never to take for granted the partnership we share and the purpose You give us together. The words "thank you" don't come close to expressing the depth of gratitude I feel toward You for this experience of loving and holding the man You have brought to me. Please help me to do my very best to uphold him in all the ways that will please him and You.

IN YOUR GREAT NAME I PRAY. AMEN.

I WILL CHERISH OUR UNION

He who loves his wife loves himself. For no one ever hated his own flesh, but nourishes and cherishes it, just as Christ does the church.

EPHESIANS 5:28–29 ESV

Marriage—and God's holy plan for it—is a sacred gift with physical and spiritual ties. And with such an inexpressible gift comes the responsibility to treat it with the utmost care. Whatever we treasure is what we will go beyond normal limits for, to make sure it is protected, nurtured, and loved. Jesus demonstrated how much He cherishes us—His church—by physically dying on a cross and instilling His spirit into us. The world calls us to put our own wants and needs and desires before others, but Paul puts a husband and wife's love on the same level as the Savior's love for us—a level that is far above and beyond anything else we desire. It's that important to God and, hopefully, will always be that important to us.

Father, I am grateful for Your love for me. Our relationship is a treasure beyond measure, and I thank You every day for it. I want to uphold and cherish my husband the way You uphold and cherish me. I pray that he will feel valued to the highest degree and that our marriage will be blessed with Your favor as we nurture each other and grow together. Please convict me when I think only of myself and put my wants above his. Give me patience during the times when he thinks only of himself, so that we can come together and trust we have the other's best interests at heart, the way You have our best interests at heart. Thank You for the immeasurable love You show and for blessing and keeping us in it.

IN YOUR PRECIOUS NAME. AMEN.

I WILL TRUST AND RESPECT YOU

I have trusted in Your faithful love;
my heart will rejoice in Your deliverance.

PSALM 13:5 CSB

Trust and respect. Those are big words. Saying you'll trust or respect another human being is a big commitment, but doing both—while *knowing* there will be times of testing—is enormous. They are actions that often require proof of worthiness, and are absolutely vital for peace and harmony to exist in a relationship, especially in marriage. The only One any of us can completely trust and respect—the only One who is completely worthy of both trust and respect—is Jesus. None of us are perfect. That means none of us are 100 percent worthy, so, what is a wife to do? She can look up, hold tight to her trust in God, and remember to cover her husband with grace. In turn, remember that he'll have his moments to do the same in return.

Father, trust and respect seem like such simple words, but they are so difficult to give. Please give me the desire to freely trust and respect my husband. Help me to trust him with big and small decisions. Help me to give him the benefit of the doubt even when I feel skeptical. Help me, Lord, to respect him as a man of God. Help me cherish the ways that You made him. Give me eyes to see him as a child of God, fearfully and wonderfully made. Give my husband the confidence that he is a man worth trusting and respecting.

IN THE NAME OF JESUS I PRAY. AMEN.

I WILL LAUGH AND CRY WITH YOU

[There is . . .] a time to weep and a time to laugh; a time to mourn and a time to dance.

ECCLESIASTES 3:1, 4

There's nothing like a friend to share good times and good laughs with. What's really telling, though, is whether that same friend will cry with you when times are tough. Not all friends will willingly walk into your pain to grieve with you and do so without judgment or a time clock. And it's an exceptional thing for that friend to be your spouse. A lifelong commitment of sharing inside jokes and celebrating joyous occasions is only as good as when the valleys and setbacks are shared as well. Having setbacks without the joy makes a marriage lopsided at best. Both are blessings that are very much needed for bringing balance and wholeness to two united hearts.

Lord, You know that when my husband is downcast, my heart breaks. I often feel helpless. Give me the depth and courage to be a support when he's grieved. Help me to get close and carry some of his burden and mend any brokenness he feels. Whether or not I understand what he's going through, help me to be present and available. I want him to know that he is not alone and that what hurts him hurts me. I also thank You for the times we share in laughter and joy. Please protect all the ways we can enjoy each other. Help us make time to "dance" physically, spiritually, and emotionally. Help us both to remember that You made varying emotions for us to share.

ALL PRAISE BE TO YOU. AMEN.

I WILL BE FAITHFUL THROUGH GOOD TIMES AND BAD

[Eve] took some of its fruit and ate it; she also gave some to her husband, who was with her, and he ate it. Then the eyes of both of them were opened, and they knew they were naked.

GENESIS 3:6–7 CSB

It's easy to be faithful during good times in life, but when the heat comes, when faced with bad times, every marriage is tested for its durability. Look at Adam and Eve. They had the perfect life together, and through a series of bad decisions, their lives changed for the worse. They were driven out of their home—the garden—and had to work through their new direction in life together. They didn't split up and go their separate ways because times got tough. The big difference between humankind then and now is that today when followers of Jesus call on God, we have the gift of His Spirit in us to forgive and to heal, to strengthen and to cover all that we do with His grace. His faithfulness to us is our call to be faithful to one another—through good and bad times.

Lord, You know that trials and temptations will come. I know that I am not beyond making a mistake or following my pleasure instead of what You tell me is good. Help me be tethered to the strength of Your Spirit and resist temptation. Help my husband to find strength from the same source. Help us, as a couple, to continually pursue goodness and truth and the options that You say are wise. God, You will ultimately give us the strength to resist temptation and to forgive when someone else wrongs us. Help me to be a wife who loves to forgive and show mercy.

THANK YOU FOR BEING MY SOURCE.
AMEN.

I GIVE MY HAND AND HEART

Two are better than one because they have a more satisfying return for their labor; for if either of them falls, the one will lift up his companion.

ECCLESIASTES 4:9–10 AMP

We all need help at some time or another, and what comfort it brings to know beforehand that the help will be there without conditions or strings. The only way for that to happen is for love to be at the core. To promise your hand—with your heart in it—is as close to being like Christ as a person can get. Being on the receiving end is certainly a blessing, but serving Christ side by side can be the most fulfilling activity a husband and wife can experience. The Lord reaches and upholds us with His righteous right hand, so doing the same for our partner in life is a holy honor worth repeating.

Lord, when my husband's hand reaches for help, let mine always be there to hold it. When he falls and struggles to get up, let my arms be there for him to hold onto. When he can't see which way to turn, let my love be a light that steers him toward You. When he is discouraged, let my heart fill his with the truth of Your compassion and grace. When he feels misunderstood, let my words be wise and bring the encouragement he needs. To the best of my ability, help my hands and heart to be an ever-present source of comfort, strength, and joy in his life. I'm so grateful You brought us together. Please bind us together through the mountaintop highs and the valley floor lows. Keep us and hold us near and dear to Your heart.

IN JESUS' NAME I PRAY. AMEN.

FROM THIS DAY FORWARD

Because of the Lord's faithful love we do not perish, for His mercies never end. They are new every morning.

LAMENTATIONS 3:22–23 CSB

A couple's wedding day is hopefully a day that neither one forgets—lest the "doghouse" becomes occupied! Not just because it's the day they become husband and wife, but because it's *the* day their vows are stated before God and witnesses. And while that day is generally a specific date and year, it can also mean *today*, right now. "This day" is renewable every day of marriage, the way God's faithful love is pledged to us not just once but every day—it's ongoing with each new sunrise. His mercies in marriage never end, and hopefully a husband's and wife's mercies toward each other will never end either.

Lord, Your faithful love is a source of security that I have come to rely on every day. Likewise, I want the faithful love I have for my husband to be a source of security for him. Renew in him this day and every day the commitment I made to him to do life together within the bounds of Your love, which is limitless. Help me to keep and honor him with meaning and purpose on our anniversaries, as well as on all the days in between. Let each year be a mile marker that reveals a stronger, greater, more impenetrable bond than the year before. Thank You for Your faithfulness to us, and help us to remain faithful to each other.

IN YOUR GRACE AND MERCY I PRAY.
AMEN.

AS LONG AS WE BOTH SHALL LIVE

I will confirm my covenant with you and your descendants after you, from generation to generation. This is the everlasting covenant: I will always be your God and the God of your descendants after you.

GENESIS 17:7 NLT

As long as we both shall live . . . ." Could you imagine this part of your wedding vows ending with "for as long as you don't blow it"? Or how about "to be redetermined every year on our anniversary"? No! That would be like God saying we are forgiven and have eternal life with Him . . . unless we sin again. What would be our incentive to receive Christ as our personal Savior if He put conditions on us from the start? We—the church—are the bride of Christ for as long as we live, which means forever. God's intent for marriage is to be for a lifetime. We all know that this doesn't always happen, but it is still the high and holy mark for which we aim.

Father of the universe, I feel so very blessed to know that Your love is given not only for my lifetime but for generations after I am gone. Knowing this helps me to say with confidence that I will love my husband for as long as we both live. I will always be his wife and the mother of our descendants, should we have any, with the steadfast, enduring kind of love that You show to me. I'm grateful for the grace we both have because of Your Son's sacrifice. Help me to carry Your torch of grace into my marriage day by day, year by year. Bless and keep us in Your hands as we have and hold each other in all the seasons of life You have planned for us.

IN YOUR GREAT NAME I PRAY. AMEN.

BEARING THE FRUIT OF HIS SPIRIT

The fruit of the Spirit is love, joy, peace, patience, kindness, goodness, faithfulness, gentleness, and self-control.

GALATIANS 5:22-23 CSB

Ripe fruit in any season is a pleasure to enjoy. Whether fruit is on a vine or in a person's character, it takes proper pruning, seasonal fertilizing, consistent watering, and a lot of time—but it's worth all the effort. The Spirit of God in us offers access to our own personal training ground for developing His fruit, not only individually but together within marriage. Sometimes a husband develops faster in an area than his wife and vice versa, but when love remains first and foremost, there is room for God's grace to fill any gaps. Over time, it's rewarding to measure growth by comparing how you acted—and reacted—a year, two years, even five years ago with your actions and mindsets today. Through His Spirit, Jesus is constantly transforming a husband and wife into His image—a gift only He can give.

Lord Jesus, I pray for the fruit of Your Spirit to grow and be evident in our lives each day. Expand our love not only for each other but for our family, for our friends, and for people who don't know You. May we know Your joy as our own, regardless of circumstances. Help us to walk in Your peace that passes all understanding, especially when we struggle to understand why things happen as they do. Help us develop patience—in times of waiting, with others who challenge us, and with each other. Increase our awareness to be kind in our actions and good in our thoughts and motives. I pray that my husband's faithfulness to You will remain steadfast and increase with time. May his gentleness be a blessing to others around him. And enhance his ability to control and discipline these traits in a way that blesses him and glorifies You.

ALL PRAISE BE TO YOU. AMEN.

STRIVE TO UNIFY

[Jesus] told [the Pharisees], "Every kingdom divided against itself is headed for destruction, and no city or house divided against itself will stand."

MATTHEW 12:25 CSB

When countries go to war, it's normal for people to gather together to build forces to protect their land and to protect their freedom. Unfortunately, when couples are divided in thought and have separate agendas, they too often fight each other rather than join together to fight for the greater cause of their marriage. Unity is vital for the long-term staying power that's needed for couples to succeed. But how do you get and maintain unity? It begins by taking our eyes off ourselves and turning them to what God has to say. It means remembering what has been mutually agreed on and letting that be a starting point for the power of His Word and Spirit. Sometimes it means letting go of what we want for the greater cause of love.

Lord, I understand the importance of having unity in our marriage and in our home. Without it, we can't withstand the constant forces that try to wedge us apart. Please keep our focus on You and Your Word for our hope, guidance, timing, and wisdom. Put a hedge around us to keep deceit and misconception from coming between us. Make our home a safe place where my husband can voice his concerns about areas where he doesn't feel unified. Please give us both a determination to take steps toward Your divine will for the way we live. Give him discernment over the things that can cause division or that are already a problem, and help us talk and pray about solutions. Please make us stronger and more joyful in our relationship and in our home. And most of all, bring us closer to You.

IN JESUS' NAME I PRAY. AMEN.

WORK AS WORSHIP

We are His workmanship, created in Christ Jesus for good works, which God prepared ahead of time for us to do.

EPHESIANS 2:10 CSB

Many of us struggle to experience joy and fulfillment in the work we do. There can be boredom, tasks that we just don't like to do, a boss who micromanages, and coworkers who rub us the wrong way. When even one of these irritants is present, work can feel like drudgery. It's hard to accept that God prepared us ahead of time to do what we do, yet He did. And if we sincerely trust Him and want to please Him, we can look at whatever vocation we're in (whether a CEO, a restaurant manager, or a parent) as a means to an end—*His* end for the fulfillment of His purpose, not our own. When work is viewed as a vessel of His love for us, we can do it with a whole new attitude of grace and humility, gratitude and praise.

Lord, I lift up my husband and the mountains he faces each day as he works. Bless his heart with the parts of it he likes, and cover him with Your grace in the areas he doesn't. Help him to see You at work in the places where You want to teach him, challenge him, and reveal his capabilities to him. Equip him to do what You have called him to do, one day at a time. Turn his outlook on the work before him into worship toward You. Guide his thoughts, his hands, his feet, his voice into the fulfillment of Your purpose for his life. Deliver him through his worldly trials into Your heavenly promise of provision and prosperity.

ALL PRAISE BE TO YOU. AMEN.

WHAT IT MEANS TO SERVE

Show hospitality to one another without grumbling. As each has received a gift, use it to serve one another, as good stewards of God's varied grace.

I PETER 4:9–10 ESV

We live in such a "me first" society, don't we? It almost seems foreign to think of putting others first, especially when we don't feel up to it or it's inconvenient. Then there are the minor—or major—irritants that cause us to place conditions on any help we might give to our neighbor, let alone our spouse. And when we think of showing hospitality, it's natural to automatically think of our neighbor, but the place where it begins is in the home with the ones we love. Serving our spouse is of utmost importance in both our marriage and our spiritual life.

Lord, I come to You with a humble heart and ask that You show me how I can best serve my husband today. Help me to put aside any differences we have and serve him out of the love I have for him as Your child. I have my own ideas about what to do, but I want to get "me" out of the way so I can see his needs and wants through Your lens. Help me to be a sounding board for his stresses as well as his dreams. Highlight ways I can help him and lighten his load. Give me ideas for how to help brighten his mood and lift his heart in a way that makes him feel loved and appreciated. Make me a good steward of Your grace by serving him in ways that are meaningful to him. If he asks me to do something I don't feel like doing, help me to picture You washing the disciples' feet—something You did with love even though it seemed beneath You. Help me to keep love at the core of my motives as his wife. Thank You, Jesus, for being the ultimate example of what it means to serve.

AMEN.

COURAGE TO STAND FOR TRUTH

Beware of false prophets, who come to you in sheep's clothing but inwardly are ravenous wolves. You will recognize them by their fruits.

MATTHEW 7:15–16 ESV

There are so many ways the world tries to deceive us, get us to believe lies, and compromise our faith. Unfortunately, even some Christians can misguide, mislead, and stray from God's Word for the sake of popularity and attention. This is easily done by changing one word in a Bible passage or taking portions out of context, so if we aren't familiar with what God Himself says, we set ourselves up for trouble. Husbands and wives are called to filter anything they hear—whether at church, at work, at school, on TV, or social media—through the truths in the Bible, and to seek God's guidance together through prayer.

Father, I know some people are sly and clever at taking Your truths out of context and doing what they can to mislead us. I pray an extra protection over my marriage and over my husband in this regard. May we not fall prey to anyone's deceit. Give my husband discernment when he's at work or going about his daily tasks to recognize falsehoods, however small. Give him the courage to speak Your truth into situations that might lead him or those around him into doubting their faith or the love You have for them. May he be brave enough to gently call into question a friend's attitude or action that is contrary to what You would have him do. Your Word is a light to our path, and I pray it shines brightly each day we are alive so we can serve and glorify You.

IN YOUR GREAT NAME I PRAY. AMEN.

YOUR BODY, THE TEMPLE

Don't you know that your body is a temple of the Holy Spirit who is in you, whom you have from God? You are not your own, for you were bought at a price. So glorify God with your body.

I CORINTHIANS 6:19–20 CSB

The human body is an intricate part of God's creation. No two humans are alike—on the outside or on the inside. Each one of us is uniquely made for the Holy Spirit to dwell within. That's an amazing concept! And that's why it's so important to take care of ourselves physically, emotionally, and spiritually. When one thing is out of balance, the body suffers. When our body suffers, our relationships suffer. God wants us to do our best to care for our body so that we are the most efficient and effective for being ready and able to share His love with others, beginning with our spouse. To think that our body is "the temple of the Holy Spirit" is enough to motivate us to take great care in what we put in it and how we treat it—all for His glory.

Lord, I'm humbled to think of my body and my husband's body as the temple for Your Spirit. It's important to You that we care for our physical condition as much as our spiritual wellness. Help us both to honor You in what we eat, what we drink, and how much we exercise. The daily temptations to indulge in food and drinks that rob us of energy and vitality are very real. The busyness of our schedules makes it too easy to skip meals or eat convenient, unhealthy food and feel depleted or bloated at the end of the day. May Your Spirit in us empower us to create a healthy balance and choose wisely regarding nutrition. We want to thrive and serve You to the best of our ability. Make us constantly aware that You are not only with us but also in us, and that is a gift.

THANK YOU, JESUS. AMEN.

TURN AND SEE

Jesus turned and saw her. "Have courage, daughter,"
He said. "Your faith has saved you."
And the woman was made well from that moment.

MATTHEW 9:22 CSB

No matter who Jesus was with, He had a desire and supernatural ability to look past the surface of who the person portrayed herself or himself to be and zero in on the real person underneath. He didn't assume anything based on outward appearance but instead looked deep in the heart of the person and spoke directly to the condition that her heart was in. In this verse, He first turned toward the woman at the well, then He saw her. She was a Samaritan, and Jews in that culture didn't speak to Samaritans, especially in broad daylight. But He was intent on satisfying her thirst for truth, and He gave it. It takes courage for us to intentionally turn toward those we'd normally avoid, but He gives us the courage we need to do just that. For the sake of His kingdom, He turned and saw.

Father, I pray that You will use my husband to minister to others. I know You can and do use him at times he doesn't even realize, because You are constantly working in people's hearts and lives. Please give him the desire and the courage not to avoid someone who may be difficult or different. Give us both the margin in life to take the time to look and discern what's beneath the surface of a happy or sad face and speak truth to them in ways that bless them and honor You. I pray that Your Spirit will give us the right words and actions needed for spreading Your love to others. Show me how I can help and encourage my husband as he grows in his faith and becomes bolder in his witness for You.

FOR YOUR GLORY I PRAY. AMEN.

NEVER TOO YOUNG OR TOO OLD

The righteous thrive like a palm tree
and grow like a cedar tree in Lebanon. . . .
They will still bear fruit in old age,
healthy and green.

PSALM 92:12, 14 CSB

Nowhere in the Bible does it say we're too young or too old to be effective for God. We often think that if we're too young and inexperienced to do a traditional job, we have no purpose. Likewise, when our lifelong job ends, we think it means we are no longer useful to society. That would probably be the case if our identities were in our jobs. But when our identity is in Christ, we are His workmanship to be used how and when He leads, no matter our age. Abraham was one hundred years old when Isaac was born. Mary was between twelve and sixteen years old when she gave birth to Jesus. Paul served the Lord until he died, and while he was a tent maker, he was first and foremost a servant of Christ. Our age and job may affect what we do, but they aren't our identity.

Lord, I pray on behalf of my husband and for the purpose You have placed on his life. Regardless of his age, education, interests, and accomplishments, I sincerely believe You can do miracles through him—I pray he believes this as well. You have blessed him with amazing gifts and talents that make up who he is and provide the help he needs for serving You. I pray that no person or thing can get him to think any less of himself during times when life doesn't go as planned or certain doors don't open his way. Help him to remember that what he does is not who he is—that he is Your child, Your creation, and You love him. Thank You that we have each other to remind us of our true identity, and that is in You, not this world.

PRAISE AND LOVE TO YOU. AMEN.

HE IS HIS STRONG TOWER

Lead me to a rock that is high above me,
for You have been a refuge for me,
a strong tower in the face of the enemy.

PSALM 61:2–3 CSB

It's nothing less than amazing when you go to a place high above street level, such as the Empire State Building or the top of a mountain, and are removed from the noise, the hustle, the obstacles, and the urgency to get from one place to another. It's an experience that not only provides cleansing but also the perspective that we lose by being down in the trenches of our everyday work. Jesus ascended to mountaintops to spend time with His Father and renew His strength. Sometimes it's impossible to physically go to a high place for refuge, but one can always stop and look to the Lord from deep within and receive His strength, His grace, His perspective, and His care. He is our mountaintop. He is our high-rise. He is our rock in the face of our enemy.

Lord, I lift my husband to You—his rock, his high place, his strong tower—for refuge. May the height of Your love be the cleansing breath he needs. Let it flow through him and carry reminders that You love him, You are in control, and that with You, he can look at each day with victory. Renew within him the strength he needs and instill in him a boldness of heart that will keep him from being shaken by anything. Give him Your eternal view for the twists and turns he must navigate to accomplish Your will. Hold him steady in Your hands and steadfast in his faith in You.

ALL PRAISE BE TO YOU. AMEN.

JOYFUL AND WILLING

Restore to me the joy of Your salvation, and make me willing to obey You.

PSALM 51:12 NLT

There are many seasons of marriage that might not feel joy-filled. There are seasons of tension, illness, fear for a child, or uncertain next steps. But through every season and decision, we have a choice to realign our hearts to God or turn away. We get to decide if we will let the joy of following Him lead us into obedience. This obedience will naturally affect our marriage. It will lead us to love our spouses as Christ loved. It will lead us to sacrifice for our spouses. It will lead to a work ethic that finds joy in serving our families through even the most menial tasks. But a willingness to obey isn't born from obligation or duty; it is rooted in the knowledge that our God sent His Son for us. This willing obedience allows us access to the ultimate joy!

Lord, help me to love my husband out of a place of joy. Help me to prioritize my obedience to You and follow the commands You've given me to love and serve my husband faithfully and frequently. Please give my husband a love for You that is also rooted in his salvation. Help my attitude in our home and in our marriage to bring him joy and comfort. Help him to be transformed by Your love and Your gift of salvation. And help us to knit our lives together with the truth of Your grace. Thank You for the opportunity to experience true joy apart from our circumstances.

IN THE SAVING NAME OF JESUS
I PRAY. AMEN.

JUST THESE SIMPLE THINGS

What does the Lord require of you? To act justly and to love mercy and to walk humbly with your God.

MICAH 6:8

Sometimes in the daily shuffle of life, it's easy to forget what God asks of us. We get lost in the highs and lows of creating a home, raising kids, planning for the future, searching for free time, and trying to connect with our spouse. Micah 6:8 sums it up well, though. The Lord requires you to act justly, love mercy, and walk humbly with your God in *all* areas of life. Think about the practicality of those requirements in your life, specifically in regard to how you love your husband. Do you help him fight for justice in his life? Do you dole out mercy to him, offering forgiveness and grace at every turn? Do you choose humility, admitting that you are wrong sometimes and need help and instruction? Don't let small everyday worries obscure the larger calling of your life. Infuse your life with justice, mercy, and humility—all for the sake of honoring your Lord.

Lord, thank You for my husband. Thank You for the gift of his love and presence in my life. I pray that my love for him would reflect what You ask of me. Help me to fight for justice in his life. Help me to fight for him, support him, and be on his side. Help me to be merciful toward him, using compassion and understanding and love as my first response. Help me to approach him with humility rather than pride. God, I pray that You would draw him to the same sort of life—a life that reflects what You ask of Your children. Help our marriage to be one that honors You.

IN YOUR MERCIFUL NAME. AMEN.

ALL OF YOU

Love the Lord your God with all your heart and with all your soul and with all your strength.
DEUTERONOMY 6:5

As we come to the close of this devotional journey, remember that love is ultimately what will anchor you to both your Savior and your husband. You will be presented with so many things to love in life: your children, your friendships, your collectibles, your clothes, your appearance. There will be no shortage of people and objects to give your love to. But early in Scripture, God reminds us that we ultimately will find the most joy-filled, purpose-filled life available if we offer all our love to God. As we learn to love God with unrelenting tenacity, God will reveal to us how to love others in this same way. He will transform our desires and our sinful natures. He will cleanse us and make us the people He desires us to be. Continue to anchor yourself to the ultimate example of love: a God who sent His own Son for you. As you continue this journey with your husband, remember that this Source of love will be the most satisfying love you have to offer. Love God with all your heart, all your soul, and all your strength.

Lord, You are a good, good God. Thank You for loving me in a way that I do not deserve. I pray today, Lord, that You would help my husband feel Your love. Help him to experience the overwhelming goodness of Your presence in his life. Help him to love You without hindrance or distraction. Help him to find satisfaction in You and be tethered to Your love and Your purpose for his life. Thank You for the gift of marriage and that You constantly use it to make me more holy. Thank You for the process of becoming more like You and for the gift of getting to love my husband so deeply.

THANK YOU, LORD. AMEN.

TOPICAL INDEX

DaySpring

LIVE YOUR FAITH

Dear Friend,

This book was prayerfully crafted with you, the reader, in mind. Every word, every sentence, every page was thoughtfully written, designed, and packaged to encourage you—right where you are this very moment. At DaySpring, our vision is to see every person experience the life-changing message of God's love. So, as we worked through rough drafts, design changes, edits, and details, we prayed for you to deeply experience His unfailing love, indescribable peace, and pure joy. It is our sincere hope that through these Truth-filled pages your heart will be blessed, knowing that God cares about you—your desires and disappointments, your challenges and dreams.

He knows. He cares. He loves you unconditionally.

BLESSINGS!
THE DAYSPRING BOOK TEAM

Additional copies of this book and other DaySpring titles can be purchased at fine retailers everywhere.